THE THOUGHTFUL LEADER

The Thoughtful Leader

A Model of Integrative Leadership

JIM FISHER

UNIVERSITY OF TORONTO PRESS
Toronto Buffalo London

© University of Toronto Press 2016
Rotman-UTP Publishing
Toronto Buffalo London
www.utppublishing.com
Printed in Canada

ISBN 978-1-4426-4798-5

∞ Printed on acid-free, 100% post-consumer recycled paper with vegetable-based inks.

Library and Archives Canada Cataloguing in Publication

Fisher, Jim, 1942–, author
The thoughtful leader : a model of integrative leadership/Jim Fisher.

Includes bibliographical references and index.
ISBN 978-1-4426-4798-5 (hardback)

1. Leadership.   I. Title.

BF637.L4F57 2016   158'.4   C2016-901908-X

University of Toronto Press acknowledges the financial assistance to its
publishing program of the Canada Council for the Arts and the Ontario Arts
Council, an agency of the Government of Ontario.

Canada Council   Conseil des Arts
for the Arts   du Canada

Funded by the   Financé par le
Government   gouvernement
of Canada   du Canada

Canada

ONTARIO ARTS COUNCIL
CONSEIL DES ARTS DE L'ONTARIO
an Ontario government agency
un organisme du gouvernement de l'Ontario

To my students, from whom I learned so much
To Mary, who keeps me grounded

CONTENTS

THE THOUGHTFUL LEADER

Chapter One

INTRODUCTION

Life can only be understood backward, but it must be lived forward.

Søren Kierkegaard

This book will help you learn to be a better leader by being more thoughtful about what leadership is, how you are expressing it in your daily life, and how you exercise it when needed. It is written from a lifetime of immersion in the subject, first in my role as a management consultant, advising and observing leaders in the public and private sectors; then as a business executive in both corporate and operational roles; and later, for nearly two decades, as a teacher of leadership to MBA students and mid- to upper-level executives at the Rotman School of Management at the University of Toronto. Like most things in my life, this immersion was not planned or intentional. It just happened. In fact, when I started my career, I would have said that leaders are more likely to be born, not made, and that leadership was more about character than learnable skills. It was only in the teaching part of my life – interacting with students from around the world, younger and older, in all kinds of enterprises – that I came to find a more practical and useful definition and understanding of leadership. The more I learned, the more convinced I became that leadership is actually a teachable skill. It is a skill that involves deep thought more than gut instinct. This how-to book is one that I wished was there when I was in the trenches, responsible to shareholders for their capital and to thousands of hard-working people for their welfare. This is a book that I wished I had when I was advising leaders as a management consultant.

I believe that everyone has within themselves the capability to lead if they only know how to break the idea of leadership into understandable chunks and then integrate it back into a more powerful whole. I didn't always believe this. Until I became a teacher, I believed that leadership was mostly about character and intrinsic ability. When I was chosen for leadership roles growing up, in school, and in the business world, I assumed that it must have been because I had those special gifts – but don't ask me to define them. I now know that this is not the case. If I was chosen for leadership roles and if I had some success in those roles, it was through a combination of luck and intuition. How else can you account for the fact that I had both successes and failures? If my gifts were so special, what would explain the failures? And what would account for the success of many people with far different characteristics and abilities? I now believe that it is more important and far more useful to consider what to do with the skills and personality you have than it is to try to develop skills and traits that do not come naturally to you. I look back on my life and understand why certain actions engendered responses that I had hoped for as a leader and why others did not. I see the missed opportunities because I was not more aware of what leadership is all about. I believe that the ideas in this book will help others make fewer errors and let fewer opportunities slip away. To be clear, this is not a book about leading like me. It is about how you and those around you can become better leaders on their own. I believe that everyone will find their life more fulfilling if they are able to lead others when they feel strongly about something. And, because I believe in the essential goodness of people, I believe that the world will be a better place if people lead where they see the need.

The Thoughtful Leader

The book is called *The Thoughtful Leader*. The title draws its inspiration from the work of Daniel Kahneman and Amos Tversky. These eminent cognitive psychologists changed the way that experts in many fields think about how people behave and make decisions. Kahneman was awarded the Nobel Prize in Economics for their joint insights into economic decisions, largely inventing the field now known as behavioral economics. Unfortunately Tversky had passed away and Kahneman had to accept the award alone, sad that he could not share it with his colleague. Kahneman captured the essence of much of their work and made it accessible to a wide audience in his bestselling book, *Thinking Fast and Slow*. The simplified idea is that we deal with the world through either the thinking fast part of our brain, which enables us to respond to people and situations as they arise, or the thinking slow part of our brain, which more carefully considers how we might respond to people and situations to arrive at an optimal outcome. The thinking fast skill gets us through the day but is prone to influence and error. Using the thinking slow part of our brain is more likely to avoid errors but takes more effort and is tiring.

As I reflected on how leadership is practiced, I could see how these two influences manifest. The "leadership moment" – coined by Wharton's Michael Useem in a book by the same name – is a moment that arises randomly and unpredictably. It is the moment in a meeting when someone says or does something that is, in your mind, completely off track. Or it could be a moment when someone says or does something that is completely on track in your opinion but is being ignored or rejected by the group. It is the moment when someone on your team asks a tough question or directly challenges your position. It is the moment when the meeting with the boss or a customer or a peer takes an unexpected turn. These moments require an immediate response. Do you let them go by or do you intervene? If you intervene, what do you do and how? We all want to form a response that is thoughtful and measured, but there is no time to reflect. The thinking fast part of the brain springs into action. We all intuitively recognize that the spontaneous response to that leadership moment could well turn out to be more impactful than all of our carefully scripted, shaped, and rehearsed moments. But there are so many things to consider. How important is the issue of concern? Is it an opportunity to create a coalition around a bigger agenda or is it just a one-off? Is there a principle-based way of intervening? If you intervene this time, on what basis will you be able to intervene next time? Is this moment an opportunity to move things forward or is it a moment to respond to a threat?

These legitimate and natural concerns trigger a range of emotions in all of us. Kahneman and Tversky warn us that our emotions will color our thinking fast response. Our response may well be way off base. The opportunity will be lost. The wrong message will be sent. The thoughtful leader is one who has put in the time and hard work (thinking slow) to develop a model of leadership that will influence the spontaneous (thinking fast) response, increasing the chances that it will lead to a more desirable outcome. The thoughtful leader has an agenda and is looking for opportunities to move it along. The thoughtful leader is conditioned to look for and recognize "leadership moments" that often define that leader. This book will provide a framework for organizing what can sometimes be a bewildering number of contextual considerations into an orderly agenda.

Leadership Is for Everyone

Leadership happens all the time and all around us. It happens in organized settings – government, business, and social enterprises. It happens in clubs and teams and families. And there have always been leaders. In organized settings we may call them kings or popes, generals or chiefs, presidents or chief executive officers. But in any setting, there has always been the person who steps up when the group is drifting or uncertain or just needs a clear direction. And because leadership is so important in a functioning society, we have always accorded power and status to those who take on, or are given, the mantle. People with ambition and drive strive for the power and status of leadership positions. They are usually only too willing to accept the trappings and accolades that come with leadership. If this is the case, why does the world need another book on leadership? There are two reasons. The first is that we all have experienced the fallout from ambitious people who achieve a leadership position and then fall short – failing to meet the expectations of the role. Poor leadership leads to failed organizations and unhappy people. Time and again, through my own eyes and those of my students, I have seen the impact of poor leaders; most frustratingly, I have seen how easily they could have become much better leaders and produced much better outcomes by doing a few things just a little bit differently. But there is a second, perhaps more important, reason for this book. I suspect there are many who would step up and take on leadership roles if they believed that they could do it. The attraction of power and status is not enough to overcome their lack of confidence in their own leadership abilities. I believe that there are many with great ideas and great intentions who let the world pass by when they could be making it a little better. And I believe that the world would be a better place with their contribution. Many people live a life of regret because they don't step up to lead when they see a better way. Trusting as I do in the essential goodness of people, I believe that a world where people are able to lead where they see the need will be a better one. There is no finite amount of leadership needed in the world. Wherever and whenever something could be made better by rallying people to make a difference, there will be an opportunity for leadership.

Thinking About Leadership

In the fall of 1998, after working for decades in a variety of roles in a number of North American businesses, I was asked to teach an Executive MBA class for the Rotman School of Management at the University of Toronto. The course, called Human Resource Management, was about the various elements of an HR department in any enterprise: hiring, job descriptions, compensation, assessments, development programs, and the like. At the time, there was no course on leadership at the Rotman School. Very few business schools had a course on leadership and fewer still had it as a required element of a program. Most had a class or two on leadership within a course on human behavior. Even the word "leadership" was not used as it is today. Conceptually I could see describing the practice of leadership as "managing humans so that they become a resource." But what was that practice? Throughout my life I had led, either by choice or by nomination, in minor situations where I knew the people and interacted with them every day. In my career as a strategy consultant I worked with many senior people in the private and public sectors – people whom today we would call leaders. Then, as an operating executive for over a decade, I had been given responsibility for increasingly larger operations spread over progressively wider geographic areas. I was responsible for a dairy that served a large region – the heavily populated south of the province of Ontario. I was responsible for a chocolate bar company that covered Canada, with a few pockets of exports, but with most of the employees at the plant and headquarters in Toronto. Then, for several years, as president of George Weston North American Bakeries, I was responsible for thousands of people across North America, in three time zones, who worked 7 days a week, 24 hours a day. In sum, I had experienced the sensation of being a leader and had observed others being leaders, but what did I observe and what did I experience?

In retrospect, I have lived through a significant evolution in leadership as we think about it. Early in my career, when "leadership" was not a word in common usage, I saw "the boss" as a manager who was knowledgeable, direct, and controlling. People in organizations did as they were told and generally gave the organization their full commitment and loyalty. Following the social turmoil of the sixties, people stopped doing what they were told. Loyalty gave way to managing one's own career, and leaders were called on to be visionaries. In the public and the private sector, for-profit and not-for-profit, every organization had to have a vision statement. Although people were less inclined to the blind obedience assumed in the leader-as-manager era, they were prepared to commit to an organization that had a meaningful purpose. Leaders were people with vision who could motivate, not direct. Today, as the world becomes more global and more diverse and moves faster and faster, people want to have more influence on where their organization is going. They are not content to wait for a visionary leader to show the way. Leadership today means finding a way to engage and channel the energy and talent of every person in the organization.

In this journey, leadership has gone from rarely mentioned to the center of any discussion about how things are done or how we – as a nation,

an enterprise, or a group – will meet any sort of challenge. We have become fascinated with leadership: what it is, what it does, what it takes,
why it is important. And there is good reason for this fascination. The
most successful enterprises today are built on the foundation of empowered, committed people throughout the organization, people who step
up to lead when and where necessary. As organizations become larger,
the world becomes smaller, and everything happens faster, leadership
happens in many different situations and in many different cultural con-
texts. As technology continues to shake the foundation of long-accepted
business models and practices, this means leading in situations where
direction from the top is not likely to be helpful or timely. Leadership
has never been so important, nor has it ever been more difficult.

As well, the whole concept of leadership has changed significantly.
The old model of the boss at the top of an organization setting the direction for all to follow is far too limiting for the globalized, fast, diverse,
and, frankly, far more interesting world we live in now. Unlike in the
world that supported the great-person theory, today's most effective
organizations don't rely on finding the gifted few to be nurtured and
developed. Today's most effective organizations are moving far too
quickly to wait for the great person at the top to make all the necessary
decisions. Instead, they call on people at all levels to lead within their
own sphere of influence. They rely on people stepping up where they
are needed to make things happen. Today, it is more useful to focus
on what leaders do that can be taught, rather than on who leaders are
or the traits that they might possess. It is more useful to think about
people acting as leaders in some circumstances and as followers in others than to think about leadership as a static position or rank. And it is
more useful to think about those who do hold those ranks or positions
developing leaders and encouraging leadership in others, instead of
always acting in some singular leadership role.

Connecting Theory to Action

But in this new "discovery" of leadership, which has given rise to tens
of thousands of books, we've somehow lost sight of what we want

leaders to do. Many of the books and theories on leadership focus on how leaders direct, inspire, motivate, empower, engage, or reach the heart. Too often, they miss one crucial reality: *we want leaders to get results*. What we want from leaders is more revenue or higher profits, software that works, schools that perform, agencies that deliver, and hospitals that serve. In the real world it is about meeting the monthly budget, or dealing with a customer problem or a talented but difficult colleague or an angry union. It is about meeting quarterly targets and customer satisfaction metrics. It is about reacting to a disruptive technology or to a new competitor. Leaders make good things happen; otherwise, they don't get to keep their jobs and continue to be called leaders. Effective leadership starts with a person who has an idea about how to make the enterprise (or the division or the department or the group) achieve the needed results and who then puts the idea to work, encouraging people to change their methods and to put their hearts and initiative into getting that something done. All the motivational, empowering, directing, inspiring, engaging ideas have to be about this simple reality: leaders are only effective (and thus earn the label "leader") if they have a winning idea and are able to implement it. A really effective leader can do even more. A really effective leader can get results *and* build the capability of individuals *and* build effective teams so that results are achieved even beyond the moment, the incident, or the project that is the focus of a leadership action. But they have to get results, or they don't stay leaders.

If it sounds like a hard job, that is because it is. Leading others is the most difficult job anyone can be called upon to do. The job requires a great deal of thought. The reason it is so difficult is that it requires the simultaneous integration of many elements, often in real time: an insightful understanding of the material situation; an appreciation of the skills, biases, and needs of the people to be led; a deep understanding of the leader's own biases, shortcomings, and strengths. Along with this is a need to reconcile all the ideas and theories about leadership and what leaders do. Is it about choosing one set of theories over another? Is leadership situational or universal? Is leadership about who you are or about what you do? Is leadership a set of behaviors or a set of actions?

How important is style? The fact is that leadership is about a lot of different ideas in the context of many different situations. Leadership is contextual and complicated. We need a simple framework to think through all this noise and confusion.

I did not find a way through the confusion in any of the popular theories or leadership books. The road to a successful leadership course and the idea that leadership is thoughtful work came through two separate inspirations: (1) Daniel Kahneman and his insight into how our brains function, captured in *Thinking Fast and Slow*; and (2) Roger Martin and his insight into integrative thinking, captured in *The Opposable Mind*. I have already cited Kahneman and his research partner, Amos Tversky, who inspired the title of this book. Roger Martin's work provides the inspiration for the subtitle: *A Model of Integrative Leadership*. His observation is that while we all develop models of the world which simplify its complexity and make it manageable, there is a developable skill – integrative thinking – that enables some people to create more sophisticated and powerful models. His meta-model of integrative thinking led me to search for a model of how leaders act – what they actually do – to integrate the various elements that make the job so challenging and ultimately so rewarding.

I will develop and explain this model of integrative leadership: a model of leadership as practiced, or what leaders do to create followers who are useful followers in a fast-changing world – energized, active, initiative-seeking followers. The model integrates three existing and accepted models of what it takes to get work done: a model for managing people; a model for providing direction; and a model for engaging them. I will describe each model from top to bottom and show how they relate. Then I will show how each of their parts connect to one integrative model and how that model integrates the salient elements of leadership – the leader, the situation, and the people to be led.

The next chapter will give an overview of three models of leadership and show how each grew out of the previous. Chapter 3 will show how these models can be seen as parts of an integrative model of leadership, pictured in a 3x3 grid, where each row and each column has its own internal logic and where each box relates to the others. The next three chapters will delve deeper into each of these partial models to draw out the nuances that must not be overlooked in the integrative model. Chapter 7 will explore the dynamics of the model and the linkages that work across each of its elements. Chapter 8 will show how a leader has to integrate many perspectives, considering there are many groups and constituencies to lead. While the book focuses on the practice of leadership, some essential skills are required to be truly effective. Chapter 9 will explore some of the more fundamental capabilities that can be cultivated for more effective leadership. Chapter 10 has a few closing thoughts on how the integrative model can be used in a variety of situations.

Leadership today is difficult, but I remain very optimistic about the state of leadership in the world. Those with ambition and courage who are already leading can be better. Those with great ideas can take the leap and make the world a better place. Those who see small ways of making a difference can step up and be that difference. I look forward to all your contributions.

Chapter Two

LEADERSHIP MODELS

The job of getting people really wanting to do something is the essence of leadership.

Dwight D. Eisenhower, September 1955

Leadership is an intense human activity that encompasses what can seem to be a bewildering array of elements. Making a difficult management decision while considering the impact on the people affected and balancing that against your own hopes and anxieties can feel overwhelming. It is no surprise that many fall back on a simple formula, such as when in doubt show strength, or when in trouble call on the team, or when the answer isn't clear act like Jack or Meg or Howard or Sheryl or whoever was the hero of the last leadership book you read. We all know that there has to be a better way. The job is too complex to rely on a simple formula. But what is this better way and how do we find it? This was the dilemma I faced as I put together that Executive MBA leadership course. How do I bring the theories of leadership to life in a way that does not oversimplify their application but at the same time avoids making them so complicated that they cannot be effectively used? How do I give my students something that will be real and useful in the various phases of their careers as each faces problems with which I have no familiarity?

Fortunately I arrived at the Rotman School at the same time that Roger Martin was arriving to become dean. He had been persuaded to leave a very successful career as a strategy consultant with Monitor Company, at the time one of the world's pre-eminent strategy firms, to take on a new role. As anyone who knows Roger would expect (and I knew him well from working with him in my own strategy consulting firm and then using him as an advisor in my operating jobs), he took on the biggest challenge facing management education. Academic management research and teaching is done in the silos of specific academic disciplines: economics, finance, accounting, marketing, strategy, operations, and human behavior. But there are no interesting or meaningful management situations that can be solved in a silo. All management activities cut across the academic disciplines. A marketing decision has to be made in the context of the corporate strategy and within the overall economy, with an eye to operating results and what can be financed. This fact is second nature to managers and not unknown to management educators. Educators use a variety of methods to cope with it. Some believe that case-based teaching is the answer because the problem is always described in the context of an overall situation. However, that is only a partial answer, as all cases are influenced by the particular silo-based concept being taught and the "lessons learned" will be drawn from the academic discipline of the individual teacher. Some believe that the answer is a "live case" field study that sends students off to solve a real problem, drawing on the concepts from the various courses they have completed. Again, this offers a partial answer: it relies on the students themselves acting as the integrators without any overarching concept. Some have experimented with cross-discipline team teaching, but there is no reason to believe that an academic, steeped in a single discipline, will be particularly adept at integrating with other disciplines.

Roger set out to find a better way. His approach was to invite to the school a number of interesting, demonstratively successful individuals from a variety of fields to be interviewed live and on stage. He did not want a prepared speech because he wanted to probe what and how they were thinking when they made tough choices. What was A.G. Lafley thinking when he asked the greatest consumer products research lab on earth – Procter & Gamble's own – to reach out for ideas from anyone anywhere? What was Isadore Sharp of Four Seasons thinking when he set out to create the world's leading high-end hotel chain by eschewing opulence and grandeur and focusing on personal service. What was K.V. Kamath of ICICI Bank thinking when he set out to disrupt the banking industry in India by offering customers personalized service? What was Piers Handling thinking when he set out to create in Toronto what is now the world's most important film festival, TIFF? What were they thinking? And more important, how were they thinking?

As Roger looked for his meta approach to the integrative thinking problem, I attended these sessions to get material for my leadership course. Isadore "Issy" Sharp is famous for his visionary leadership and for building a business on values: the golden rule, paying attention to even the lowest paid and least skilled person – all the stuff of leadership theory. But I could not help noticing that he was also a fundamentally strong businessman with great insight into his customers, smart marketing, and a wise approach to financing. And this was true of others. Lafley is famous for his vision-led and values-driven approach at P&G. He is famous for his ability to spark a remarkable wave of innovation in an old company operating in old product segments. But he was also the person who rebuilt the confidence of the financial community by delivering reliable quarterly results. It was clear that I was looking for integrators in the leadership sense, whereas Roger had taken on the far bigger job of looking for an underlying concept that would have universal application, that could be taught, and that would make our students more effective when they went into the workplace. His meta concept would provide a framework for a leadership-specific application.

Integrative Thinkers Are Complex Model Builders

Systems dynamics guru John Sterman of MIT has long observed and taught the insight that we all make our way through life by constructing mental models. No one can cope with the vast array of data and information that we receive every hour and every day. Fortunately we don't need to. Instead, we simplify the world by building mental models of how the world works. That way we need to deal only with the deviations. We hear these models expressed regularly: "If you want peace, prepare for war." "Early to bed and early to rise makes a man healthy, wealthy and wise." "You only get out of it what you put into it." "Service is the highest calling of mankind." Models are useful and necessary but they can be dangerous. When we build a mental model we leave out some things that we don't think are important and emphasize others. Models simplify reality, and they are sometimes wrong. Nations that prepare for war may get drawn into conflicts they would have avoided if they were not so heavily armed. Perhaps it is better to be prepared to work into the night if you want to get wealthy. Sometimes we put a lot into something and come up empty, whereas other times we do things without a lot of effort and get a lot from them. And perhaps giving is more important than service. Models are useful but they are not reality. We need to be constantly aware of that distinction. The trick is to construct a model that is sufficiently complex to accommodate what is important and yet simple enough to be useful.

Roger's insight, captured in *The Opposable Mind*, is that the people he was interviewing were unique because they had become masters at building these models, models that were complex enough to include more of the salient variables and with a more sophisticated insight into causality and a deeper understanding of how the parts connect. Further, these masters of integrative thinking were unwilling to accept the simpler models that resolved a problem by accepting some kind of suboptimal compromise. *The Opposable Mind* is a clear and readable exploration of this phenomenon. Even better, it breaks out the steps one can take to become a better model builder, a better integrative thinker. It is also a call to create a model of integrative leadership.

Toward an Integrative Model

Leadership is complicated – a perfect "wicked problem," to use a currently popular phrase. A leadership model has to contain enough of the salient elements to capture the complication. It has to satisfy all the biases of the operating executive: that real work has to be accomplished, budgets met, orders out the door, people hired and fired. But it has to take into account all that that we know about the power of ideas to bring people together. And it needs to consider that people want to feel their work matters and to have an opportunity to contribute. The leadership model also has to handle the reality of an ordinary working day, where leadership is not just about being the CEO running the entire enterprise but applies equally to the more mundane but essential task of working within an organization to get things done: getting human resources to solve a problem; getting the software developers to deliver useful programming for a new service offering; getting the operations group to adapt production to market needs; and getting a project team to come to a conclusion.

Effective leadership also requires an understanding of causality at the operating level: if we take this action, our competitors are likely to do that; if we increase service levels, our customers will respond this way; if we develop an integrated information system, we will receive these benefits but will lose these features of adaptability and customization. These are normal management questions, which are hard. Leadership is harder. Leadership requires a deep understanding of people, at both the individual and the group level. What behaviors are needed to implement a management plan? What behaviors are likely when a particular management approach is taken? If budgets are tightened to get costs in line, how will people react? Will those with surpluses start hoarding? Will people make the easy cuts or make the hard choices? Is there a way to take a management action that will induce desired behaviors? What causes certain parts of the organization to always get support for their projects while others wait in line?

Leaders also have to think about how everything comes together – what Roger calls the architecture of the integrative model. Being an effective leader requires implementing simultaneous action in specific areas without losing sight of the whole. The leader who wants an empowered organization cannot just let that happen without thinking through how the empowerment can be directed at the most pressing problems and opportunities. There may be a great opportunity for a rousing call to action and the words may come naturally, but if there is no way to put the plan into action, then perhaps the words should not be spoken.

Finally, effective leaders are not satisfied with partial solutions and compromises. They want a winning strategy right now, but they also want an organization able to deliver, adapt, and improve over time. They want an organization that works today but is also becoming more capable for tomorrow. They want strong individual contributors as well as an effective team. They want a solution that will work today and will also build the foundation for what has to be accomplished when the next problem or opportunity emerges.

The Leadership Model – An Integrated Grid of Action

As I began to teach various elements of leadership theory, I found myself constantly answering questions about how all the theories fit together. My students forced me to become an integrative thinker about leadership, to understand the importance of salience, causality, architecture, and resolution. They pushed me to develop the leadership grid presented in this chapter, and for the past decade, they have given me the opportunity to see how they use it in many different situations.

The grid has three main elements: *managing*, as defined by academics and practitioners over many years; *directing*, for which I use the terminology made famous by John Kotter; and *engaging*, which requires a deeper understanding of human motivation. In the rest of this chapter I will summarize those models and explain how they are interrelated. In subsequent chapters I will go deeper into the specific models.

Model One: Managing

Both individuals and groups need to be managed. It is nice to think that a great inspirational speech will galvanize everyone to take the right action at the right time, coordinating with everyone else, but it rarely happens. Meetings need agendas and follow-up. Team members have to know their assignments and deadlines. No one can get caught up in leading without considering the imperatives of management.

Chapter 2 will set out a more complete description of managing, how it fits with other elements of leadership, and how it was created out of the work of Henri Fayol. For now we can simply acknowledge the well-known management cycle – Plan, Organize, Control – which is familiar, even intuitive, to everyone who has been given responsibility for any kind of organized activity.

The Familiar Managing Cycle

Managing implies a "command and control" mindset. It implies a scientific approach to work. Be clear what has to be done. Make sure everyone knows their job. Set SMART goals, and don't forget to follow up. This idea of management is taken from our early models of effective organization – the church and the military. The managing cycle starts with the creation of a plan, which sets out what has to be done and by when and considers the various elements that have to come together to accomplish the goal. The next step in this cycle is to assemble the people, assign tasks, teach people how to do those tasks, and specify the processes for getting the work done. Finally it is important to keep track of the work as it progresses and to measure the final product against the goals, targets, or objectives that were initially set. And it is a cycle because there is feedback between the steps. If things aren't going well, reconsider the plan, add to or change the group, or adapt the process.

Think about the steps required to operate a fashion retail chain. Wherever I go in the world I see Zara. Zara is part of Inditex, a fascinating and highly successful operator of fashion retail outlets including Zara, Massimo Dutti, and others. The goal of the Inditex chains is to have affordable but up-to-the-minute fashionable clothes in its stores around the world. To ensure that its clothes meet current fashions, it follows the unique practice of making clothes in small batches, mostly in the Iberian Peninsula and mostly within days of their direct shipment to the stores. This is in sharp contrast to the approach of most apparel retailers, who anticipate fashion trends a year ahead, make clothes in large batches in Asian factories months before each season, and keep them in large warehouses for seasonal restocking of stores.

Figure 2.1. Model One: Managing

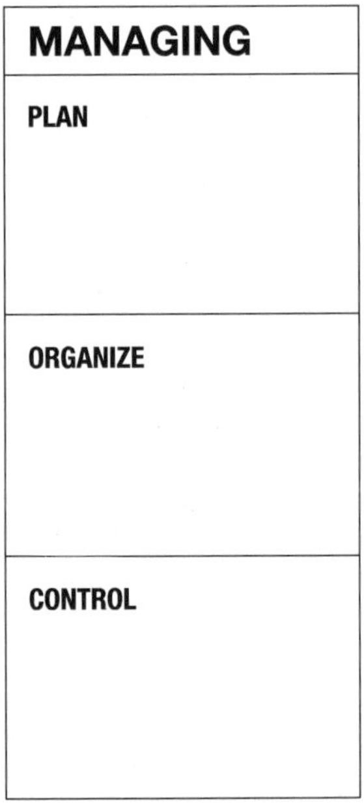

MANAGING
PLAN
ORGANIZE
CONTROL

Zara's system requires a process for mapping out where the great trend-creating fashion events happen and ensuring that the right people with the right attention to detail are there, keeping up with the latest styles. Zara requires a number of tools to succeed: a system for collecting input from the fashion-conscious people working in the stores; a process for assimilating all these ideas and deciding which ones to include in the collection; and a process for sourcing the materials and producing the patterns, specifying quantities, colors, and sizes. Factories have to be found that can make the clothes at the right quality level, the right cost, and the right time. Systems are necessary for informing stores about what is available, for processing orders, for shipping, receiving, merchandising, and keeping track of the money. Retail is detail. It is a long and complicated system that needs careful management – plan, organize, control. Whenever I walk into a Zara store I imagine all the steps taken to have the assortment seen there and I never cease to be amazed.

The managing cycle is not just for the giant enterprise. It works – and is followed – whenever a group gets together to accomplish a task. Any small team operating to take on a very quick project will follow the same cycle: developing a plan to achieve the objective; assigning tasks and determining how and when to measure results; keeping track, following up, and adapting the plan and/or the work assignments. One thing I have observed in the classroom is that people from all types of work situations recognize and intuitively follow this managing cycle as they go about their work. It seems to be the natural way to behave. The teacher has a plan for the day, the week, the term, and the year. Assignments are handed out, tasks assigned, and work evaluated. The principal in the office and the administrator at the regional level both work within the managing cycle. The nurse manager in a busy hospital will have recognized technical expertise in science but will also be an intuitive expert at planning, organizing, and controlling. The principal researcher for a large global project to discover part of the mystery of cancer follows the same cycle of activity. And none of these people had to go to business school to learn it. It has become engrained in the way that we do things.

Limitations of the Managing Cycle

In a sense the managing cycle contains everything needed to have people get work done, the essence of what any leader attempts to accomplish. In fact, one might ask, why do we need to go further? The problem is that over time and in many workplaces, managing as practiced comes to place emphasis on detail, process, and science. As organizations become bigger and more complex, managing systems develop more and more rules. Planning becomes an annual event, a necessary precursor to the approval of annual and quarterly budgets with specific measurable targets for groups and individuals, even if the rhythm of the business does not really lend itself to annual cycles or to quarterly reporting periods and even if what is really important does not lend itself to simple repeatable measurement. Some enterprises operate in an industry of constant change, where plans and responsibilities should be adjusted frequently. Others operate in a longer time cycle, in which it is important to keep the distant goal in mind and not adjust annually, where pushing expenditures back and forth across a fiscal year end to meet some artificial target is simply not productive. Organizations do need structure and defined responsibilities, but the mechanics of defining jobs, assigning tasks, and specifying decision-making processes are inevitably too slow and cumbersome to keep up with today's demands, which require businesses to adjust to unanticipated changes in the environment with the attendant emergence of new problems and opportunities. Control systems often end up emphasizing what can be counted, not what is important. Bonus programs can often be gamed and always have unattractive steering effects.

Even that small team working on one quick project can fall prey to the same problems. A plan is put together before there is a real understanding of the purpose and context of the project. Roles and tasks are assigned without a common agreement on the end to be accomplished. Follow-up tends to focus on what is easy to count, not on what really matters. It is a sign of the times that many of my students are involved in IT projects, putting together systems that will deliver the right information to the right application at the right time in the right format. I cannot tell you how many times they report on their experience of working on projects where no one knows the total context of the project, where progress is measured in lines of code and the end result is a system that does not come together to meet the needs of the end users.

Model Two: Directing

The managing cycle is a powerful tool but a limited one. The need for flexibility to adjust to a changing world was felt intuitively by influential executives like the legendary Jack Welch, the CEO of General Electric for 20 years. During his tenure, General Electric remained one of the largest and most successful businesses in the world, at a time when companies in similar industries were struggling to compete. Academics such as John Kotter at the Harvard Business School and Michael Useem of Wharton analyzed how to go beyond managing. Welch, Kotter, and Useem, each in his own way, recognized that in a world of rapid and unpredictable change and increasing diversity, organizations needed something more than the managing cycle, useful though it may be. There must be a way of directing people that connects them to a larger purpose.

In 1990, John Kotter published his now famous article "What Do Leaders Really Do?" After surveying the wreckage of "well-managed" companies in the 1980s and the emergence of true powerhouses from that same decade, he concluded that really effective executives were not just managers. They did something else; Kotter called it leading but I call it directing, as I believe there is more to leading than the elements in his model. Nomenclature aside, his model is a significant addition to the management cycle model. In chapter 3, I will explore Kotter's ideas in more detail and show how they made a critical contribution to contemporary thinking about leadership.

Start with Vision

Kotter started with vision, the idea that in a world of change, where plans can never keep up with events, it is important to have a compass, a central idea of what the enterprise is trying to achieve. Zara is the idea of Armancio Ortega and Rosalia Mera, who always knew they wanted to provide affordable fashion to women leaving the home and going into the workplace. They wanted women to feel empowered by feeling good about how they looked at work. Sam Walton wanted Walmart to give working families in the bottom half of the economic spectrum the products they coveted at prices that they could afford. Jack Welch of General Electric wanted to create a company that had the power of a large corporation and the agility and aggressiveness of a small company. A.G. Lafley wanted to make Procter & Gamble a consumer goods innovation powerhouse.

Some say "it all starts with a dream." In a bestselling book called *Start With Why*, Simon Sinek captured the powerful idea that we are more effective if we know why an action is required. The job of the leader is to articulate the why, the vision, the reason we should care about the work to be done. And it is not the job of just the CEO or the founder to have a vision. It happens everywhere. The IT specialists working on a

Figure 2.2. Model Two: Directing

DIRECTING
VISION
ALIGNMENT
MOTIVATION

software project will be more effective if they know what the project is intended to accomplish and if the vision is articulated in a way that is meaningful to the team. Is it a quick fix to a problem or the foundation for more substantive change? Is it aimed at solving the problem of one business unit, or is it an opportunity to build connectivity across the enterprise? A school principal working in a public system, surrounded by teachers and administrators and rules and process, can choose to be an administrator, finding replacements for sick teachers, watching the caretaking budget, and ensuring that the paperwork is completed. Or that same principal can choose to be a leader with a vision of what that school can mean for the children, the families, the community at large, and the community of teachers.

Creating a vision is hard work and often personally risky. Every vision includes some desirable outcomes and excludes others. Visions embody aspirations that may not be met. Visions can be seen as idealistic dreams, scoffed at by those who see themselves as hard-headed realists. Leadership is hard, thoughtful work.

Build Alignment

Directing starts with an idea that can be articulated as a vision or statement of purpose. It begins with a lot of thought and care. It is hard to come up with a vision and commit to it. And once the vision is there and crystallized it becomes even harder! The vision goes nowhere if it cannot be effectively sold to others. The next hard job of leadership is to be able to articulate the vision, to find the words that capture the idea and the courage to be "out there" and take a stand. Every vision statement includes some things and leaves out others. Every statement sets out an ambition, a bar against which the courageous leader will be assessed. Leaders are people who want to accomplish something and are not afraid to say so.

Leaders must become communicators, using whatever style or forum they find most effective. And this communication has a purpose. Leaders need to get people aligned to the vision, understanding it, seeing its possibilities and limitations, and ultimately agreeing that the vision articulates the best way forward and that they want to be part of the journey, challenging though it might be. Alignment says that it is powerful for people to know, understand, and agree with the vision or purpose of the enterprise. Alignment is a reminder to think about all the people who have to be led to make any initiative successful. Alignment means that people need to understand and agree with the vision, not just know what it is. Alignment recognizes that any vision needs to be sold, not just told. Alignment is about commitment, not acquiescence. It takes explicit, thoughtful effort to achieve the commitment that comes from alignment. Leadership is hard, thoughtful work.

Find Motivation

Alignment is critical but it is not enough. Leaders understand that to get people to change they have to find a way to motivate them. They need to do more than know the direction and agree on it. It takes effort to change anything. Think about setting out to lose weight. You have a vision of yourself 10 pounds lighter. You are aligned with the idea that you will be healthier and look better when your vision is realized. But are you motivated to keep walking by the cookie plate, to resist the late-night trip to the refrigerator? Leaders pay attention to the range of elements that motivate changes in behavior: a feeling of belonging, an increased sense of self-worth, an opportunity to grow as a person, and perhaps some tangible reward – a bonus, a chance for a promotion, or just a pat on the back.

Anyone trying to lead, to get people to really want to do something, will recognize that there are many ways to motivate people. Although a good deal of management theory focuses on economic motivation, many more motivators exist. And it's a good thing because in many situations, the putative leader simply does not have access to economic motivators. Few people get to design the salary and wage grid. Fewer design the bonus structure, if there is one. Most people working in the middle of an organization have to work with those systems as they are and to find other ways to motivate: an opportunity to contribute to something meaningful, recognition, a chance to grow, or the approval of those from whom approval is welcome. These are all tools that a thoughtful leader can and will employ. Leadership is hard, thoughtful work.

Kotter's Influence

When Kotter's article appeared it gave rise to the now-familiar saying "what we need is more leaders and fewer managers." It gave new clarity to Peter Drucker's observation that managers do things right but leaders do the right thing, as if there were a clear split between leading and managing, one done at the exclusion of the other. But, in my mind, Kotter's most important contribution was in making it clear that leading is work, just as managing is work. Leading is not about charisma and presence. No one needs to be told that creating plans and budgets, organizing people to get things done, and measuring and following up are hard work. Kotter gave us the insight to recognize that articulating and communicating a vision is also hard work. Taking the time and making the effort to align people to a vision is work. It is also work to think through and then activate the elements that motivate changes in behavior. But that distinction does not mean managing and leading are not inextricably intertwined. The fact is that we can find the elements of Kotter's leading work in each part of the Managing model.

Managing and Leading Are Linked

All plans have within them an implied (or stated) vision or sense of the ultimate goal or purpose of the enterprise. But as the plans become more rigid and applied to calendar periods, it becomes increasingly important to extract the vision from the mechanics of the managing cycle. Plans with targets, benchmarks, and performance improvements are implicitly built on the belief that an enterprise's environment is relatively stable and that its real purpose is to outcompete. Plans filled with new initiatives are built on an implicit belief that the environment is changing and that the enterprise has to keep changing to survive or to get ahead. Too often though, in the mechanics of putting the plan together, these fundamental beliefs and aims are lost, or they are mentioned but then overwhelmed by the immediate action steps. The idea in the Directing model is to break out the vision – the end purpose, the aspiration that the plan itself is intended to further – and make it explicit and meaningful. Since the vision is what makes work meaningful, making it clear has a powerful effect that is lost when it is subsumed under the details of a plan.

Similarly, one could say that all organizing work is really intended to ensure that people's activities align with the ultimate purpose. The mechanics of job descriptions and organizational arrangements create the start of alignment. If an international enterprise has a vision based on adapting the product or service to local needs, then the structure is usually built around country groups. If another international enterprise has a vision built around global products, then it organizes itself around global product groups. If an enterprise is focused on efficiency, it will be organized by function with clear hierarchies and controls.

If an enterprise is focused on adaptation, new ideas, and responsiveness, it will be organized in a way that encourages teams, collaborations, and structures with very short lives. The *organize* step is directed at achieving very specific alignment. By taking the implicit message buried within managing's organization designs and making it explicit, it is more likely that the desired effect will be realized.

Finally control systems are put in place to ensure that the enterprise achieves the specifics that will bring it to that ultimate purpose. Control systems *motivate* specific action. "What gets measured gets managed." Control systems respond to our need to know if we are succeeding or by how far we have fallen short and how far we need to go. They are often tied to bonus systems that emphasize the motivational part of the managing cycle. But there are other, far more motivational opportunities than just the achievement of a measured target, even when those opportunities do not carry the possibility of a bonus. Extracting the motivational aspect of control from the mechanical ensures that appropriate attention is paid to the more indirect, sometimes subtle, but often far more powerful motivational forces that actually induce people to act.

Since managing and leading are so inextricably connected it is far more useful to think about them together.

In our world of constant and unpredictable change, the Kotter model contains within it the really useful idea that leadership is work, which is definitely an improvement on the idea that leadership is mostly about special traits. It pulls out the elements needed to keep an enterprise or a group working together on those things that really matter. It provides guidance about what has to be planned. It offers a yardstick for assessing the efficacy of organizational arrangements. The model reminds us that control systems should be aimed at what matters, not just at what is easiest to count, and that, in any event, measuring and rewarding work together as a means of motivation.

There is often a debate about whether someone can be a leader and not a manager, or vice versa. And there is even discussion about whether being a manager detracts from one's effectiveness as a leader. This debate goes back to the tendency of many to see the world in the "either-or" frame. Either one spends time grinding out the detail and discipline

Figure 2.3. A partial model of leadership

MANAGING	DIRECTING
PLAN	VISION
ORGANIZE	ALIGNMENT
CONTROL	MOTIVATION

of managing, or one spends time in the inspiring world of leading. Some refer to this as the classic CEO/COO division of responsibility. The fact is that it is not an "either-or." Kotter himself wrote about how the two elements – what he called "leading" and "managing" – have to work together. Jack Welch of GE, in many ways the model of the modern corporate leader, could be seen every day in the trenches managing: going over plans, searching for and developing talent, following up on performance. At the same time, Jack, in his own words, "never passed up an opportunity to sell the vision." If we go back to Eisenhower's definition, "getting people really wanting to do something," managing is an essential part of defining what is to be done. Directing ideas gets at the "really wanting" part of the quote. The directing elements speak to the need to articulate and sell a vision, to get the alignment and motivation that gets the work done well.

The Unity of Vision and Action

Michael Useem at Wharton is clear that leadership involves the best of both the Managing model and the Directing model. Useem has a simple and powerful way of describing the essence of the idea. In his view, effective leaders were characterized by their ability to create a unity of vision and action. One without the other just does not get the job done.

Perhaps this quote illustrates it best:

A vision without a task is but a dream
A task without a vision is drudgery
A vision and a task is the hope of the world

This famous verse, said to have been found inscribed in stone in an eighteenth-century English church, expresses a profound and timeless thought. When we have a job to do and are aligned with the purpose of the work, work is a pleasure: *the hope of the world*. When we are given a job but without any reason for doing it, the work *is drudgery*. When we hear a great vision but no one picks up the tools to implement it, it is an empty promise, *but a dream*. Combining the models is far more powerful, useful, and realistic than believing that one contains more truth than the other.

Model Three: Engaging

Managing tells people what to do. Directing tells them why they are doing it. These are powerful ideas when combined. But there is more. Managing and directing still imply an "all seeing, all knowing" someone who is in charge of where everything is going. Today we need a workforce that feels that it can and will redefine the future. Today we need people who are really engaged in their work.

It can be hard to function in a world of complexity and uncertainty. Through most of my working life, the commonly accepted mantra was that business hates uncertainty. Governments were exhorted to provide stability so that sensible investment decisions could be made. Today, though, we all accept that unpredictable change is normal. This "new normal" provides a real challenge to leadership models one and two, which, at their essence, attempt to provide stability and order to the working condition. In a world that may never again be characterized as stable and orderly, leaders need workers who are truly engaged and prepared to respond and react when needed, not just when asked or told to. Leaders need to find a way to provide direction with flexibility, with a sense that there is a better way. We need a third model. Several decades ago, Joseph Badaracco and Richard Ellsworth wrote a book called *Leadership and the Quest for Integrity*. They set out three workable models of leadership behavior founded on three different ideas about what motivates people. They called the three approaches to leadership "Values-Driven," "Directive," and "Political." They believed that leaders should prefer one approach to another. I call those ideas "Values," "Clarity," and "Involvement." And I believe that leaders cannot choose but must work with each in an organized and thoughtful way. They are extremely useful leadership ideas.

In chapter 5 I will go into more detail about the Badaracco and Ellsworth ideas and how useful they are in thinking through how to lead.

Involvement

The Engaging model (Figure 2.4) may be more easily explained from the bottom to the top. Involvement is based on the simple idea that people want to contribute to the decisions that affect their lives. And they want to contribute in several ways. At a basic level, they want some control over what they do at work. They don't want to be told every detail about how to do their job. They want to know what is expected of them and then they want some latitude in determining how it is to be done. But a truly engaged workforce wants more. The truly engaged workforce wants to contribute to the success of the whole enterprise. If they have ideas, they want someone to pay attention to them. They want more than a suggestion box. The leader who wants to build a truly engaged workforce ensures that work is organized to allow people to use their creativity and initiative. And the leader who

Figure 2.4. Model Three: Engaging

ENGAGING
VALUES
CLARITY
INVOLVEMENT

wants to build a truly engaged workforce ensures that the mechanisms for additional contribution are clear and accessible.

Clarity

The effective leader knows that an involved workforce can be a valuable asset, finding new and better ways to do their own jobs and contributing useful ideas to the entire enterprise. The effective leader knows that people are likely to put more effort into something that was their own idea than they would into the implementation of another person's idea. But leaders also know that there cannot be chaos in an organization. People cannot do whatever they want just because it is motivating. People cannot disrupt the main flow of the enterprise for any idea they might dream up. The thoughtful work required to use the Engaging model lies in coming up with a way to shape a consensus around the leader's own agenda so that people feel that they own it and that it was not simply imposed.

Clarity, derived from what Badaracco and Ellsworth called "Directive Leadership," sets the boundaries for involvement. Gary Latham of the University of Toronto, along with his colleague Edwin Locke of the University of Maryland, developed a theory of goal setting. They posited and demonstrated that people are motivated by the challenge of meeting externally set, tough, clear goals. It is far better to set a specific goal than to just ask people to "do their best." And people are drawn to and are prone to following those people who are able to make clear, strong decisions. They look to leaders who will make the tough calls and lament leaders who leave the big questions unanswered. There is something reassuring about working in a place where decisions are timely and clear – even if they are not always what we want to hear. And it is also very difficult to be involved without some sense of the boundaries for action and the targets to be achieved.

Values

Values leadership is based on another view of motivation. The values leader knows that people want to feel that what they do is meaningful when measured against a set of principles they believe in. In the best of all worlds, they want to feel that they are working for an intrinsically good organization that does intrinsically good work with colleagues they respect. The values leader believes that people will find the right solutions to problems and that they are more likely to make the right choices on substantive matters if they are guided by the right set of values. The values leader articulates and lives those values as a role model for the organization. People follow because they feel better about themselves for being part of such a powerful social organization.

Values are what define the culture of an organization. Values can be seen as the unwritten rules about "how things get done around here." There is an endless list of values that one can choose from rather than one set of "approved" and preferred values. In some organizations the values might be about rugged independence and always keeping commitments. In another organization values could be about collaboration and helping others. As we shall see later, the choice of values is pragmatic. Effective leaders build the values that connect most closely to their vision.

Values, Clarity, and Involvement Work Together

In their book, Badaracco and Ellsworth argue that there is power in integrity, where integrity means a leader is consistent in all their actions and behaviors. They argue that leaders should have a bias for one approach and be consistent in its application. While they accept that any one of the three can be effective – and they provide strong examples of effective leadership with each of the models – they argue for leaders who have a bias for values over directive and directive over political. Put another way, they have a bias for values over clarity and clarity over involvement. In my own experience and in the thousands of stories I have gathered over the years, I find that this is neither a necessary nor a useful choice. In fact, I have found that only when the three ideas are combined are they truly effective. An organization living a strong set of values is critical. Clarity of goals and direction also galvanize effective action. Four Seasons has a clear goal of being the world's leading luxury hotel chain. Google is very clear that its goal is to assemble large user communities for advertisers by organizing the world's information. Big, clear goals are very powerful. And armed with clear goals and values, people can make meaningful decisions about their work and how to do it. They can achieve the involvement benefits of the political leader without becoming "political" to achieve it.

Google encapsulates many of its values in a simple statement: "Do No Evil." Four Seasons built its business model on the "Golden Rule – do unto others as you would have them do unto you." These statements of values are the powerful touchstones that make everyone proud to be a part of those companies. They provide an absolutely essential guide for the many decisions that are made every day, far from the oversight of the executive group. But note how pragmatically they map to the vision and strategy of the company. Four Seasons wants to be the world's leading luxury hotel chain, building on personal service. The golden rule is a great way to guide behavior in that direction. Google wants to be the world's search engine – among its other aspirations. It needs users to "Google" things because the search will be reasonably thorough with acceptable steering effects. "Do no evil" is a great way to guide people as products and services are designed and taken to market.

Values and clarity together make productive involvement possible.

Three Models Side by Side

To this point I have set out three working models of leadership, three models of how to get work done through people. I have also shown that the elements of the Directing model are buried within the corresponding elements of the Managing model. Plans are designed to achieve a purpose, which we can call the vision. People are organized to align them with the work to be done. We keep track of progress as a way to guide and motivate behavior. I also show how the elements of the Engaging model correspond to elements of the other two models.

A vision, which eventually has to be turned into a plan, is always based on some set of values. If A.G. Lafley has a vision of P&G as a company that improves the lives of ordinary people with its consumer products, there is an implied values statement that improving people's lives is a worthwhile purpose. Lafley is smart enough to know that it is more powerful to state that value rather than leave it to chance that people will "get it." Similarly people are organized to align them in a way that provides clarity to the goals that are to be pursued. And control systems ensure that people are involved in the right things, those things and actions that the leader is working to motivate.

Each model has its own integrity and internal logic, and at the same time, the models are linked. In the next chapter I will explore those linkages to show that it is a truly integrative approach to leadership.

Chapter Three

THE INTEGRATIVE MODEL

Effective leaders manage, direct, and engage. They don't choose one over another. They don't do a few elements of each; they do them all, consistently and coherently. Each of these elements requires thought and consistent action to achieve committed followers who will work together with energy and conviction. But to make this an integrative model we will have to see how all the elements interrelate.

These three models do not work in isolation. In fact they only work really well when they work together: the Integrative Leadership model. The mechanics of managing puts the emphasis on the specific work that has to get done: what my job is. The activities in directing put the emphasis on providing meaning to work: why I am doing it. But in a company like Inditex, where its people are scattered across the globe – in small groups, perhaps alone, in ad hoc teams, and in organized work settings – engaging provides the energy and the glue that holds it all together: how I should behave.

We noted earlier that all *plans* contain within them an implied or explicit *vision*. At the same time if we peel back the *vision* part of the leading model, we can see that all visions have within them an implied set of *values* that provide the unwritten guidelines on how to behave and what is important. If the vision statement is about delivering a specific kind of product, that vision statement implies a set of values about integrity, accountability, and a selfless focus on doing the right

Figure 3.1. The model of integrative leadership

MANAGING	DIRECTING	ENGAGING
PLAN	VISION	VALUES
ORGANIZE	ALIGNMENT	CLARITY
CONTROL	MOTIVATION	INVOLVEMENT

thing. If the vision statement is about customer service or experience, there is an implied set of values about consideration of others, of caring. If the vision statement is about relative ranking, there is an implied set of values about competition and teamwork and selflessness in the face of a challenge. A.G. Lafley clearly and simply explained why P&G is one of the world's great companies: it is "purpose-led and values-driven." There is a connection between the plans, the vision, and the values.

Just as organize and alignment are clearly linked, there are certain boundaries within which the team or enterprise will work. Clarity about the specific goals and targets toward which people's efforts should be directed is an essential element in effective organization and alignment. There is a direct connection between the way that an enterprise is organized, its desired alignment, and the goals that it sets out to achieve.

Engaged people are only really needed if, in fact, they are given some latitude for action – a chance for meaningful *involvement*. Controls are in place to ensure that people are achieving the desired result, which again implies that we encourage latitude and initiative in the pursuit of the goals. Control, motivation, and involvement all work together.

Working with the Model of Integrative Leadership

The leadership model captured in the grid in Figure 3.2 integrates many different partial models for "getting people really wanting to do something." Readers of leadership literature will recognize different theories and approaches: appealing to the need to be valued, to be challenged, and to make a contribution in the Engaging column; appealing to the need for meaning in the Directing column; and appealing to the need to get specific coordinated work done in the Managing column. This integrated model covers the various elements that a leader must incorporate to induce and maintain voluntary followership and can be read in any direction. Starting at the top left and going straight down, it says that for anything to happen there has to be a *plan*, people have to be *organized*, and there has to be a way to *control* the action. But hidden within those actions is another set of activities that need explicit recognition and focus. All plans are designed to achieve an end – the *vision* or purpose. All task assignments, processes, and procedures are designed to get people to *align* and focus on a specific end. And all control systems are designed to keep score in some way that is usually rewarding and therefore designed to *motivate*. Plan – Organize – Control will be more effective if this model exists within an organization that feels the power of *Vision – Alignment – Motivation*. Even within that set of activities that are labeled Directing in the chart are another set of activities. All visions or statements of purpose have within them an assumed set of *values* that the activities further promote and respect. One of the principal tools for getting alignment is *clarity* of direction and of goals and targets. And finally, it's hard to motivate people if they do not have some opportunity for *involvement*, to make their own contribution to the achievement; and, of course, there is not much point

Figure 3.2. The Integrative Leadership model: horizontal linkages

MANAGING	DIRECTING	ENGAGING
PLAN	VISION	VALUES
ORGANIZE	ALIGNMENT	CLARITY
CONTROL	MOTIVATION	INVOLVEMENT

spending a lot of energy motivating people if one does not need them to be involved in some meaningful way.

The new, integrative model puts together each of the elements found in different models of leadership. I have written them in a sequential way that roughly parallels the way that our thinking about leadership has evolved. The classical "command and control" leader of the first half of the twentieth century was a master of managing. The visionary leader of the second half of the twentieth century added the elements that Kotter labeled leading and Useem recognized as an essential accompaniment to effective managing. The inspirational leader of the new millennium reaches a dispersed and diverse workforce with the elements in the Engaging column. The three different models match three different eras of thinking about leadership. Put the three models together and there is something more powerful and universal than any one of them alone. The effective leader uses all nine boxes of the grid, and uses them consistently and supportively.

Since the model is an integrated whole, it can be read vertically to focus on a particular kind of activity – getting work done, giving meaning to work, engaging the heart. Each of the columns represents a particular aspect of the leader's work. Or, as shown in Figure 3.2, it can be read horizontally to see the connections between those elements. *Plans* serve a *vision*, which is built on underlying *values*. We *organize* to *align* with specific direction provided by *clarity*. *Control* systems ensure that the output of the *motivated* and *involved* workforce stays on track.

The model can also be seen as a whole with the interaction among all boxes, where every aspect contributes to effective alignment. The one constant that I have learned from all my students and all the places where the model is applied is that the real secret is consistency. All the elements connect and reinforce.

This book develops the model in pieces so that each element is understood on its own before being integrated as a whole. I have now worked with several thousand people who have been able, in a very short time, to understand it and see how it can be applied. It is not difficult in concept but it is hard in practice. It is not magic, nor does it require special skills, heroic qualities, or charisma; but it does require deep and careful thought. Perhaps some will apply it more skillfully than others, some more consistently than others. But anyone, at any level of the organization, with or without power of position, can do what I call "inducing voluntary followership" to channel the activities of some group of people to a desired end if they work through the model. The model builds from the concrete step of determining what specific action is required and organizing people to achieve it, to the more inspirational world of purpose and meaning, and finally to the more spiritual world of engaging. It builds on a number of theories now widely accepted in the field of leadership development.

The next three chapters break down the elements so that they can be more easily understood, followed by chapters that show how it can be used. But before we get into that level detail, the following is a story

Figure 3.3. The Integrative Leadership model: universal linkages

MANAGING	DIRECTING	ENGAGING
PLAN	VISION	VALUES
ORGANIZE	ALIGNMENT	CLARITY
CONTROL	MOTIVATION	INVOLVEMENT

from one of my students who used the framework to explain the re-markable accomplishment of a person he admired.

Shafiq's Story

(Note that the names and some specifics have been changed to protect the anonymity and ensure the privacy of the individuals in the story.)

Shafiq Agarwal grew up in Lahore, Pakistan. At an early age he entered the apparel industry working for various family companies that manufacture the T-shirts and hoodies of the great global brands. He was able to get to the United Kingdom to study at the University of Bolton, which is highly respected in the textile industry, and came back to be hired as general manager of Modern Knitwear, a family-owned company employing about 1,000 people and capable of turning basic yarn into finished goods.

Shafiq believed that Modern could become the city's largest and most successful exporter. He set out to lead. He looked at the various departments and developed plans for increasing productivity in each of them. He developed an R&D plan that would enable Modern to break away from the commodity competitors. He hired people who were specialists for each of the designated departments and made each department a profit center on its own. When that department was not busy producing what was needed for Modern's orders, they were tasked to go out and sell their capacity to other manufacturers. He set up an information system that enabled each department to keep track of its own performance, creating benchmarks for quality and productivity and flagging areas that could be improved. The departmental data was then aggregated to track the profitability of each order to improve pricing and target sales at the highest margin products.

Shafiq was clearly a very capable manager, as shown in Figure 3.4.

Modern became an impressively managed and successful enterprise. But each of the actions taken thus far could be copied and improved by other manufacturers. It would be difficult to be the city's best by just managing. Shafiq's vision for Modern was that it would be a company committed to continuous improvement in all aspects – quality, productivity, order fulfillment, and innovative products for its customers. His dream was that Modern would become the manufacturer of choice for the brands that appreciated and would pay for quality. Continuous improvement depends on workers taking ownership of their work and of the output of the factory. But to make that happen, he had to change the workers' view of themselves. They had to feel supported and appreciated by the company.

Shafiq's approach to its workforce was not the norm in the industry. He had to work hard at communicating the vision. Speeches were not enough. Posters went up all over the plant. Suppliers were enlisted with the promise of prompt payment for being part of the program. Shafiq himself walked the plant floor. His approachability and his enthusiasm for stamping out bureaucracy wherever he found it helped to align the workforce. He then added a little extra motivation with a variety of

Figure 3.4. Shafiq's model: Managing

rewards for reaching productivity and quality levels – breakfast with the general manager, dinner coupons, free apparel, small monetary rewards – all helped motivate the workforce and demonstrate the power and appeal of the vision.

Clearly Shafiq understood the key elements of leading, shown in Figure 3.5.

Using Kotter's terminology, Shafiq was a leader and a manager. He implemented a program of continuous improvement in quality and

Figure 3.5. Shafiq's model: Managing and Directing

MANAGING	DIRECTING
PLAN • Developed productivity plans for each department • Developed R&D plans to break away from commodity products • Developed sales plans to target higher margin products	**VISION** • Be the biggest and the best through continuous improvement • Put up large posters in each department • Target messages to suppliers and customers
ORGANIZE • Created an organizational structure to focus on productivity and profitability in four business units • Hired for specific departmental skills and expertise • Communicated the plan, delegating responsibility and devising systems to monitor implementation to those involved	**ALIGNMENT** • Personally take the message to the floor • Ensure that each worker is given the message directly • Seek commitments from key suppliers • Sell customers on the promise of better performance
CONTROL • Created departmental and company-wide reports • Identified deviations from standards for focused response and overall job costing to direct the sales program	**MOTIVATION** • Reward workers in a way that increases their sense of belonging and self-esteem • Reward suppliers with very prompt payments • Demonstrate high-quality and on-time delivery in return for prompt payment from customers

productivity using the classical tools of management but embedded them by paying attention to the Vision – Alignment – Motivation elements of Directing. So far, it's an impressive performance but it gets even better. Buried in those elements is another set of elements that are seldom orchestrated to their fullest extent.

The vision of continuous improvement on the factory floor and throughout the entire company contained within it a fundamental belief in the worth of each individual and the contribution that each individual can make, alone and as part of a team. Teamwork was the norm. Training and individual development were emphasized. As well as making a statement about the worth of the individual, those norms of behavior iterated the belief that women were as worthy as men. There was an explicit prohibition against discrimination. Women were encouraged to join the workforce and were made to feel that they belonged. Soon men started encouraging their wives to join the company, to work in an environment of acceptance and respect, which also vastly improved the family's overall standard of living.

Although this was an open, positive workplace, it was not soft or sentimental. The four profit centers were expected to work at full capacity and meet profit goals. When it became clear that the knitting unit could not achieve these objectives, it was closed down and the equipment sold. Funds were used to invest in further research and development. Clarity of direction and clear targets are powerful motivators.

Throughout the company, at all levels, employees felt that they had both the right and the obligation to make suggestions and express their opinions. Each was encouraged to be an active contributor to the many teams that were at work at any time. And when a department had a particularly good month, all the employees – not just the managers – were invited to have dinner with Shafiq and the owner.

What Shafiq's Story Teaches Us

The story of Shafiq Agarwal, illustrated in Figure 3.6, demonstrates all the elements of the model and the power of consistency when the elements are integrated. It integrates the traditional elements of the

Figure 3.6. Shafiq's Integrated Leadership model

MANAGING	DIRECTING	ENGAGING
PLAN • Developed productivity plans for each department • Developed R&D plans to break away from commodity products • Developed sales plans to target higher margin products	**VISION** • Be the biggest and the best through continuous improvement • Put up large posters in each department • Target messages to suppliers and customers	**VALUES** • Teamwork • Each person is valued; no discrimination • Quality and being the best
ORGANIZE • Created an organizational structure to focus on productivity and profitability in four business units • Hired for specific departmental skills and expertise • Communicated a plan, delegating responsibility and devising systems to monitor implementation to those involved	**ALIGNMENT** • Personally take the message to the floor • Ensure that each worker is given the message directly • Looked for commitments form key suppliers • Sold customers on the promise of better performance	**CLARITY** • Clear targets for each department and high expectations for performance • Extra funds are reinvested to make the company better • The drive to improve never stops
CONTROL • Created departmental and company-wide reports • Identified deviations from standards for focused response and overall job costing to direct the sales program	**MOTIVATION** • Found ways to reward workers that increased their sense of belonging and self-esteem • Rewarded suppliers with very prompt payments • Demonstrated high-quality and on-time delivery in return for prompt payment from customers	**INVOLVEMENT** • Each individual has both the opportunity and obligation to express their opinion • Walk the floor and keep an open door to create opportunities for interaction • Many teams at work at any one time

management cycle with the specific activities in Kotter's leading model. And it ties those very specifically to the engaging elements of values, clarity, and involvement. The consistency among the elements is impressive. He had a business plan for differentiating Modern from its many competitors in a very crowded industry. He had a concept of human behavior and how to get the best from each individual. He had a deep understanding of himself and how he could feel productively engaged. And he found a way to integrate each of those elements so that one supported the other. As it turned out, over the four years that my student was employed at the company, sales doubled and margins grew 50 percent. Leadership works. Thoughtful leadership works. The principles of effective leadership are the same in a textile plant in the middle of Pakistan as in a fashion retail store in Paris or a luxury hotel in Manhattan.

Chapter Four

THE HARD WORK OF MANAGING

The best way to predict the future is to create it.

Peter Drucker

Howard Schultz was a happy man. Howard Schultz is the creator and longtime head of the phenomenal global success story Starbucks. As a young man working in the coffee business, he came across an espresso bar in Milan and literally fell in love. He loved the way that the Italian espresso bar was part of the life of the people who dropped in. He loved the relationship between the barista and the customers. He loved the smell and the bustle. He set out to bring that retail experience to Seattle, then America, and then the world. His concept of creating a third home – after the house and the office – resonated. After building a business with a market value of over $7.5 billion, he promoted himself to chairman and turned the operation over to professional managers, while he became busy promoting the brand around the world, writing a book, and participating in many public activities. For many years the business kept growing. But, little by little, Schultz became unhappy with where it was going. He had this worry that the business was healthy on the top and bottom lines but that it was losing its way as a third home. He was worried about the non-coffee products that he was seeing in the stores. And Wall Street was starting to rumble that the high multiples the stock was carrying might not be justified.

One day Howard Schultz decided that he had to re-engage. He walked into a store and could not smell the coffee. All he could smell was burnt cheese. In an effort to get more revenue from existing stores, management had been adding more and more food offerings. Wanting to capture the breakfast market, they had added a cheese and egg sandwich that was heated on a grill. Inevitably some of the hot cheese ran onto the grill and produced the powerful and familiar smell. It was a successful program. But where was the coffee? Was that overpowering smell consistent with the feeling that the stores had to create to be "third homes"?

At another store Schultz found stuffed animals. When he asked the store manager about the stuffed animals, he was told by the very serious and committed manager that they had been introduced as a way to increase same-store sales. The store manager had been reading the press coverage of Starbuck's operating results and had found that growth in same-store sales was seen as an important metric. The area was saturated with Starbucks stores. He could see no other way to increase same-store sales. The manager, on his own initiative, had brought in the stuffed animals. On the one hand, it was a wonderful statement about how the employees – the "partners" in Starbucks' language – felt a real sense of ownership and responsibility to the company and how eager they were to help out where they could. On the other it was a statement that somehow the message transmitted was that stock-price-driving metrics had taken over for the customer's "third home" idea as the standard of success.

And so Schultz returned. He took up the CEO title again and set out to re-instill the vision and values of the Starbucks that he had imagined and created. On February 26, 2008, he took the unprecedented step of closing all his stores in America for a training day, during which all the staff would relearn how to make a great cup of coffee and relearn the Starbucks story. He had a giant rally of all his managers in New Orleans to retell the vision story and reignite the values that underlay a company that was as much a mission as a business. The event was a great success. The energy was palpable. Thousands of managers returned to their areas recharged and committed to the Starbucks vision and values. Schultz was drained but elated. Now he would see the results.

Over the next few months the results came in. And they were no better than they had been before the rally. Same-store sales kept declining. Earnings did not take off. New-product programs did not roll out flawlessly into the field. Sure, people were engaged. They believed in the vision. They lived the values. So what was wrong? Over the coming weeks and months, Schultz returned to the field to probe deeper. He found that Starbucks' IT systems were a wreck. Headquarters was not able to communicate with their stores. He found that the supply chain was in bad shape. They had too much real estate and the rates at which they had signed leases were too high. They had far too many people in the head office. He found flaws in the wonderful benefit programs that were offered across the company, including to the part-time workers.

Leaders Must Be Managers

A great vision and all the values that attend it are necessary but, unfortunately, not sufficient. Leaders who want to get things done have to manage. I put managing into the first column of the leadership model because it is our oldest model of leadership. Many know it as command (the plan and organize element) and control. I also put it first because it is so important to remember that leaders have to be grounded in reality. They can dream as big as they want, but they have to lead on the ground. In the end everything we want to do comes down to work! And work has to be managed. The leader who wants to be effective, who wants to actually see the vision come to fruition, who wants to make something happen, has to become a manager. This chapter will explore what that means and what aspects of managing are more critical.

The leader who wants to be effective, not just popular for a little while, has to think through the management imperatives before getting into the directing and engaging activities that are the focus of much of the contemporary leadership material. The business leader, at the enterprise or unit level, may dream of an organization of committed, engaged people delivering great customer experience and industry-leading growth; but if the competition is dominant and the resources are not there (and are not likely to be there), then it may be best to fix some problems, with perhaps a more modest vision and more restricted set of engagement tools, before stretching for the dream. The principal who dreams of leading a school with high academic achievement and a strong connection to the community had best assess the foundation before working at getting people on board for a vision that may be too far out of reach. Sometimes the leader has to be patient; always the leader has to be pragmatic.

We can all learn a lesson from Barack Obama, lauded around the world, when he swept into the White House on the audacity of hope. Hope for a more peaceful world. Hope for a world where US power was not engaged in conflicts beyond its borders. Hope for the closure of the prison at Guantánamo Bay. Hope for a more vibrant economy that would provide benefits to more of the middle class. And yet he entered the last years of his presidency with average approval ratings that were the lowest of any president since the Gallup organization instituted the measure. His vision was lofty but not delivered. After eight years with Obama as president, the world was rife with armed conflict. US power had been dragged back into the Middle East. Guantánamo Bay was still open. The income and wealth divide in America widened every day: The wealthy had never been wealthier. The middle and lower classes had made little headway. The failures may have been because the vision was beyond the capacity of anyone to deliver. He entered the presidency as the 2008 financial crisis exploded. He faced a divided Congress through much of his term. America became increasingly polarized in an ideological divide. Religious wars broke out in the Middle East. When a leader fails there are always lots of excuses. His supporters will say that it wasn't his fault, though they must be disappointed. His detractors will say that it was his fault, that his ideas never made sense.

People in the corporate world may recognize these criticisms of Obama as part of the familiar argument over whether it is better to have a brilliant strategy that is not well executed or an adequate strategy that is brilliantly executed. This is not a useful way to think. The leader as hard-headed manager needs a sense of what can be done as well as a sense of what it will take to make it happen. Visions should be a stretch to a new and better place, but leaders as hard-headed managers need to know that useful visions cannot be impossible leaps. Strategies that can't be executed with the people and resources available are not brilliant strategies. And if success is defined as brilliant execution, then the strategy must have been brilliant.

I have given many sessions to leaders in the health care industry. They are, universally, very fine people who are dedicated to improving people's lives and do wonderful work. At the same time, I find them to be the most discouraged people that I work with. After many sessions I finally put my finger on the problem. Every time I gave them an exercise using the leadership model to solve a problem, they came back with a vision statement that was some version of "world-class care to every patient who comes in the door as soon as they need it." And then they are finished and discouraged. The vision statement is wonderful but it is not grounded in reality. And the more it is promulgated, the more discouraging it is for the leader, who always falls short, and the more demoralizing it is for the workers, who become increasingly cynical as they hear the exhortations but live with the reality on the ground. If I can persuade them (and often I cannot) to develop a vision statement that is some form of "the highest quality care to as many patients as we can serve with the resources that we have available," then the lights come on. This – in whatever form it takes – is still a lofty and worthy aspiration, and its achievement is a stretch beyond what is normal in the industry, but it is possible. This is a vision that can be planned, organized, and controlled. Leaders need their feet on the ground even when their heads are in the clouds.

The Origin of the Managing Cycle

For a person working in any organization, one who needs people to achieve some specific work, the essential skill to master is known as the managing cycle. What is this managing cycle and where did it come from?

Henri Fayol thoroughly answered that question. A French citizen born in Turkey in 1841, Fayol was the son of a man involved in building a bridge over the Golden Horn, the famous deep-water port of Istanbul. In 1847 the family returned to France, where Henri entered the mining industry at age 19. Forty years later he became managing director of Compagnie de Commentry-Fourchambeau-Decazeville, one of the largest producers of iron and steel in France. It was an important position and made Fayol a man of some influence in the country. He held the position for 30 years, through the First World War, retiring in 1918. In 1916, at the age of 87, still active in the business, he wrote his famous *Administration Industrielle et Générale*.

As it turned out, his book appeared at about the same time as Frederick Taylor's *Principles of Scientific Management*. Together Fayol and Taylor are rightly famous for laying the foundations for the idea that management could become a profession (not an apprenticeship trade), that people could learn to be managers, and that management was based on fundamental principles. However, they came at the topic from completely different directions. Fayol believed that a great enterprise is built from the top down and emphasized the duties and responsibilities of those in positions of leadership. Taylor had more of a bottom-up approach, breaking down tasks into pieces and focusing on efficiency, productivity, and the elimination of waste. Both are important, but Fayol's is more informative for our study of the work of the thoughtful leader.

Fayol described the essential tasks of a manager: (1) forecast and plan; (2) organize; (3) command; (4) coordinate; and (5) control. It may not be surprising that a book written in the middle of a great war by an aging industrialist did not become a great sensation. In fact, most of his ideas were rejected at the time. However, in 1949, nearly 25 years after his death, his book was translated into English and the ideas spread. The ideas landed just as the Western world, and the United States in particular, had fallen for business schools and the idea that business administration could be taught, learned, and mastered. Following World War II, there was an explosion of interest in the study of management. Business schools attached to universities sprang up across North America. In the early days, the base of learning was to bring practitioners into the classroom to carry on the apprenticeship tradition, although some ideas from economics and sociology were added to the curricula. In the 1960s, the Ford Foundation published a report on the state of business schools and wrote a scathing critique of universities. The Foundation chastised the universities for offering graduate degrees without a foundation of conceptual theory to underpin the practitioner lessons, implying that business schools were just a cash grab not worthy of a self-respecting university. From that time, the disciplines of business education began to emerge: finance, marketing, operations, organization behavior, economics, accounting, statistics, and then strategy became recognized research-based management disciplines.

As business education continued to grow with an academic underpinning, schools began to think of management as a science. Many of the newer schools were opened as a "School of Management Science." Management came to be defined as the way to get work done through people. The basic framework for that effort became a short form of Fayol's idea: the Plan – Organize – Control management cycle. This powerful paradigm said, quite simply, that the job of the manager was to ensure that there was a clear plan in place, that people knew what their jobs were, and that there was a system to keep track of the outcomes and compare them to the intentions of the plan. Feedback loops were built into the system to allow for corrective action, to improve the plan or fix problems in the way that people were carrying out their duties. The idea was that this whole messy thing called management could be reduced to a science – scientifically (read economics) based plans, scientifically (read social sciences) derived organization, and tight (read accounting and statistics) reporting and control systems. Disciplined management became the order of the day, and awards were given to "the best managed" organizations in all fields.

The management cycle thus defined would look like this:
• The first activity is planning. Modern enterprises now put a great deal of emphasis on plans and planning systems: annual and three-year planning, budgeting, goal setting, MBO (management by objectives), working to SMART goals (specific, measurable, achievable,

Figure 4.1. The management cycle

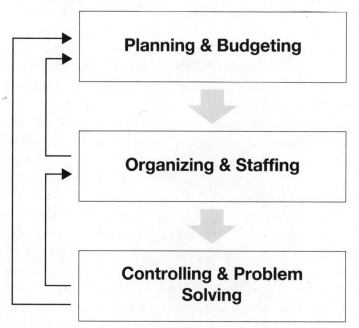

realistic, and time-bounded). Many successful organizations have developed special skills in project management with a well thought-out, methodical approach to planning.

- The second activity is organizing to achieve the plan. This involves ensuring that the right people work together in a concerted way to implement the plan and to achieve those SMART goals. This is a huge part of the work of any organization, from hiring and training to job descriptions and organization charts, processes, and approval authorities.
- The third set of activities is controlling and responding. This involves all of the measurement activities which ensure that goals are being met (final results) and that appropriate attention is paid to the achievement of milestones (key performance indicators, or KPIs), early indications that the plan is on or off track and needs to be left alone or modified.

Taken together, the three activities can then be seen as part of an integrated loop of planning, action, and feedback. Work is planned to achieve certain goals in specified time periods with specific resources. People are assembled, trained, and organized to achieve those very pointed results. Results are monitored to determine whether the people and organization are effective or whether the plan needs to be modified to reflect new circumstances.

Anyone who actually wants to lead successfully needs to master the tools of managing. Managing is the place where dreams and inspiration comes face to face with the world as it is.

The Leader as Manager

The leader at any level of any enterprise faces this challenge. It is the leader's obligation to ensure that the vision behind which people have rallied is translated into a workable plan of action. The plan of action has to be grounded in reality – the competitive situation, the resources realistically available, the urgency of action. It is not enough for A.G. Lafley at Procter & Gamble to say that "the purpose of P&G is to improve the lives of ordinary people in small but meaningful ways." It is a great purpose. It makes coming to work every day meaningful and fulfilling, but it is only a good statement of purpose – or vision – if a strategy of new products and innovation is going to be a winner. If an industry is in retrenchment but the winning strategy is quality and low cost, then another vision is needed. Howard Schultz is a great leader of Starbucks, but after everyone goes back to work determined to make the local Starbucks a third home, what exactly does that mean for hiring, training, product offerings, pricing, sourcing, and merchandising, to say nothing of developing related products like instant coffee that are not consumed in the "third home"? And if the "third home" idea has been supplanted by another consumer fad, that vision is just taking the company down a path to oblivion.

For anyone in a position of leadership, this managing business is not a second priority or something left to the operating officer. It is, in fact, an essential part of the whole. The managing ideas are the actions that bring the visionary ideas to life. For Starbucks, the design and fixturing of stores define what that home looks and feels like. The selection and training of staff define what kind of home it will be. The responsible sourcing of coffee tells the staff what values the company really believes in.

Many people looked at Jack Welch, the 20-year CEO of General Electric, as the quintessential corporate leader – the articulator of a compelling vision, the embodiment of the corporate values. But Jack saw himself as "a grunt," someone who goes home every night with a briefcase filled with plans, then gets up the next day and journeys to one division or another to go over the numbers, to assess the staff, and to ensure that targets are met. He was the essence of the operating manager. In his book *Execution*, Larry Bossidy, one of Welch's chief lieutenants and for many years the very successful CEO of Allied Signal Corporation, writes in detail about the essential role of the CEO as manager, lessons learned alongside Jack Welch.

Leader as Strategist

Beyond those simple words – plan, organize, control – what is the essence of the managing part of the leader's job? The first and most important thing is that leaders have to be strategists. Leaders have to figure out *which of the many possible paths is the one* that is most likely to lead to a successful outcome. And leaders do all that with the terrible realization that the strategy is the tangible expression of the vision. All visions are eventually translated into concrete plans through the lens of a chosen strategy. From purpose or vision to strategy to specific plans – it is all inexorably linked. The leader will work at getting commitment to a vision using all the alignment and motivational tools available. The expression of that vision in a strategy and plans had better be right. In the end, a person can do a wonderful job of leading in the sense of "getting people really wanting to do something," but if that something is the wrong something, the people, the team, and the company will be led down the wrong path. The leader will be branded a failure. Even worse, on the other side, a lot of people will be let down and bruised.

All those people who were persuaded to follow will bear the conse-
quences. They committed themselves to the vision. The vision was em-
bodied in a strategy that did not work. Will they ever trust a leader again?

Strategy development is an essential skill of leadership. The strategy
sessions cannot be empty exercises. Strategy setting cannot be simply
about paperwork and process of planning. It is at the core of the leader's role. The leader has to figure out, or find and endorse, a winning
position for the entity – enterprise, unit, district, or team – being led. In
the private sector, winning is easy to define. If the enterprise overall is
not earning more than the cost of capital, it will eventually cease to exist. In the public and not-for-profit sectors, winning is much harder to
define. The public and not-for-profit sectors are concerned with "doing
good." And there is always good to be done and not enough resources
to do as much good as could be done. In the not-for-profit sector, winning can be defined as being able to attract the resources needed to
continue to do good work. A winning strategy is one that convinces
supporters that a real need is being met and that the agency in question is meeting it better than another agency. The fact that not-for-profit
entities come and go all the time clearly shows the need for strategic
leadership to continue to find a winning position. In the public sector,
where supporting funds come from a tax base that is disconnected from
the public mission, winning is harder to define. At the extreme, a program with a losing strategy could be closed down or transferred to another agency. But that seldom happens. The leader in the public sector
does have the challenge of convincing a government or governments to
continue to fund the program at a level commensurate with the need.
More often, the leader in the public sector has to define winning in a
more inward assessment that the most is being done with the resources
available. Although this is seldom amenable to easy quantitative measures, whenever I work with public-sector organizations, they never
have trouble judging whether they are achieving as much as they can
with the resources they have available.

In any sector, effective leaders are effective strategists, conscious of the
path their organization is taking and constantly aware of whether and
how they are winning. The thoughtful leader is an effective strategist.

Leader as Organizational Architect

If strategy in the planning part of the managing cycle is the first imperative, the second is designing and building the organization. Recruiting
the right people, getting the organization design right, ensuring that
the work flow is appropriate, developing the capability of the individuals, and developing the capacity of the individuals working in teams
are indispensable requirements of leadership. As Peter Drucker has said,
"In an organization, the only thing that evolves naturally is chaos and
confusion." The leader's job is to ensure that this natural evolution
does not occur.

Two parts of the organizational architecture are most critical: getting
the right people on board and getting the right design. For many, especially those leading in the middle of an enterprise, there is seldom
an opportunity to pick and choose all the members of the team. The
leader of a project team often is assigned the people on that team. A
division or branch manager will inherit a team. It may be possible to
substitute a few people, but it is rare and very risky to try to change out
the whole team. Even the CEO of a large organization, who may appear
to have considerable latitude in selecting and keeping the best people,
will often realize that everyone can't be replaced and the group will
have to live with many of the people who are there. This reality should
not deter the leader from making a hard-headed assessment of the talent on board and from continuing the search for every opportunity to
make positive changes. But the leader as manager will recognize that
a very large part of the job is making the people who are already there
as effective as they can be. And the leader as manager will make every
effort to assign the right task to the person most able to accomplish it.

Organizational architecture is an overlooked opportunity for a leader
to make a difference. There is often far more latitude to change organizational arrangements than to make wholesale changes in staffing. I
found myself leading a large organization delivering very poor results
in the bakery business, but it was not a company that had the characteristics that naturally attract outstanding talent. It was a grinding, day-
to-day, early morning, nights, and weekends, low-growth, low-margin

business – a long way from the hyperactivity of Silicon Valley or the big money of Wall Street. In my career as a management consultant I had worked with highly educated, super-bright, internally motivated, and driven people. I knew that I could not attract people like that to the baking industry. The people that I inherited were hard-working and very knowledgeable in the industry and just wanted to do a good job. And, as I looked around the industry, it became very evident that our people were very much like the people in other companies that had better results. The quality of the people was not the issue. I stuck with the people who were already with the company, but I radically restructured the organization. It is amazing what can be accomplished when people are in the right place and where the job they are asked to do is clearly in front of them. Many people who had long served with undistinguished careers performed exceptionally when they were put into clearly defined jobs where their authority matched their accountability.

Great people poorly organized are not, in my view, a match for good people well organized. Organization means structures and jobs that are focused on the strategic imperatives of the business. Note once more the primacy of the idea that the leader has to be the chief strategist, taking ownership for ensuring the strategy is well implemented. In the case of the bakery situation, I inherited a business that was driven by regional considerations but organized as a national entity. By eliminating the national head office and setting up regional companies, the same people who had struggled within the national organization achieved amazing results. Within months, each of the regional companies had identified and implemented operational practices that turned their businesses around. Two of the regions had had no real growth and had been losing money for over a decade. Within two years, both experienced real growth and became highly profitable. Most of the implemented ideas were very small, very specific, and easily implemented; others were larger and more far-reaching and took months to realize. Together they amounted to tens of millions in annualized savings as well as substantial improvement to customer service. Objectively, one could look at all these improvements and make the case that they could easily have been achieved within the national structure. But the fact is that the opportunities either had not been seen or had been seen but not acted on. The people in the field did not think they had the responsibility or authority to make operational changes without permission. And they did not think it was worth the effort to get permission. The people in the head office were too far removed from the daily detail to see all the small things that could be improved.

The leader as manager should be aware of the often subtle impact of organizational architecture on people's behavior. When a group takes ownership for its own results – with no excuses – and does not have to ask permission to take action, it is amazing what can happen. Organization design has a huge impact on human behavior. The thoughtful leader is a thoughtful organizational architect.

Leader as Controller

Leaders have a critical role in the design and implementation of control systems. If there is any confusion about what the vision is, for some people this is cleared up by observing the control systems: "What gets measured gets managed." The connection is that what gets measured gets noticed and what gets noticed gets managed. If the leader espouses a vision of growth and entrepreneurial initiative but then monitors adherence to the expense budget more closely than the creation and execution of new ideas, people will know that entrepreneurialism is really not the vision. It is something else. If the leader articulates a vision of careful control of costs to direct scarce resources to high-priority areas but then gets excited by new ideas and does not pay attention to budgets and expense control, everyone knows that the real vision is not the one that has been articulated. Or, to put it more positively, if a leader has a vision of great customer experience and then is seen in the field with customers and in the office responding to customer complaints, everyone knows the vision is real.

One of the problems with control systems is that they tend to gravitate to those things which can be easily counted – cost per unit, same-store sales, production yields, student achievement on standardized tests, number of patients served, and results versus budget. These are all likely useful indicators of performance but many are not the most important. Even worse, anyone who works in any organization for very long will know that all measures can be gamed. "Cost per" targets can be achieved by focusing on a narrow range of "easy" products or services. Yields can be improved by producing fewer product varieties. Standardized test scores can be improved by "teaching to the test." Number of patients served can be improved by avoiding difficult patients or by being less thorough. Results that beat the budget might be a sign of good performance, but they can also be an indicator that the organization has learned how to negotiate "easy" budget targets or that there was some change in the external environment that made numbers easier to achieve.

The leader as controller will be aware of all of these problems. Certainly results have to be measured and reported. They cannot be ignored. And results are usually dominated by the numbers. The job of the leader is to put the reported results in context and to constantly look for other indications that the organization is working – or not. Do people arrive late and leave early? Is the "buzz" around how to maximize time off and overtime or about new business prospects? Is it difficult to get people to organize a charitable fundraising project or the holiday party? Do people move quickly? Do they meet your eye and smile? Are they prepared to challenge authority if something seems wrong? Control and follow-up is important. If anyone is in doubt about the real aim of the organization, the things that get noticed are the signs. The thoughtful leader is a thoughtful controller.

So in the end, managing is a critical part of the leader's job, inextricably intertwined with all the vision and alignment and motivational work. It is critical because it sets the particular path the enterprise will take to realize the vision. It is an act of great responsibility. But it is also critical because it gives concrete definition to the vision. Visions are vague but plans are specific. People align as a matter of personal choice. Organization design leads to job descriptions that are more specific. Control systems measure the hard outcomes of work. Motivation is about the energy that goes into it.

Managing brings the vision to life. And managing reminds us that leadership is about far more than being charismatic or a great motivational speaker. Effective leaders have to be strategists who can see a path to a better outcome. Effective leaders have to be organizational architects, putting together the pieces that make any kind of enterprise work – the people, the structure, the defining processes. And effective leaders know that they have to be constantly in touch with the results. Effective leaders make it happen.

When Howard Schultz returned to Starbucks, he found out that he could not succeed simply by being a visionary leader with great values who could ignite passion in his partners. He had to manage. The February 26 event and the New Orleans conference were great successes. People were energized. But by the end of the year, same-store sales were still slipping and the value of the company as perceived by outside investors had fallen dramatically. The stock price, which was $19.06 on that exuberant February day, had fallen to $9.46 by the end of the year.

Managing meant being clearer about the differentiation strategy and the concrete steps that had to be taken to achieve it. Managing meant closing 600 stores that could never be profitable and letting 1,000 people go. Managing meant going outside for expertise to replace homegrown talent that was not up to the task. Managing meant new equipment and new information technology, not just energized baristas. Managing meant paying attention to the little details that turn a vision into reality and provide clarity to those who are aligned and want to be involved.

The Power of a Vision and Management Together

In the October 1, 2012, edition of the *Huffington Post*, Sharon Vinderine described her experience going into a Starbucks: "From the moment you step through the doors, you know Starbucks has done it right … Everything is designed … to get you hooked." Vinderine details the various elements that contribute to that addiction: the aroma of the coffee being ground, from to the cashier who knows her favorite order to the barista who knows the special way that she likes it, from to the app that keeps track of her rewards to the couches for lounging. She describes an attachment that every company would like to have between

Figure 4.2. The leader as manager

MANAGING
PLAN
• Finding a winning strategy
• Setting targets and goals
• Allocating resources against the strategy
ORGANIZE
• Designing an organization that focuses on the strategic imperatives
• Assembling and developing the team
• Monitoring and adjusting the organization to deal with changing circumstances
CONTROL
• Monitoring results and reports to ensure goals are going to be met
• Paying attention to dysfunctional steering effects from controls as designed
• Devising ways to assess the commitment of the organization to the vision

a customer and their company, their product, or their service. She describes a relationship that every school would like to have with its students and parents. It is the way that every hospital would like its patients and their families to feel.

Everyone who works hard to build a great enterprise wants committed customers. Everyone who takes pride in the department or store or branch or school where they work wants that. And what is worth noting in that ringing endorsement of Starbucks are the number of elements that come into play that make it happen. Real estate had to find a place that was convenient to get to and had the room to create the desired space. Purchasing had to source the right products. The supply chain had to ensure that fresh product was available every day. The IT department had to mount the right kind of app, and the marketing group had to create the right kind of loyalty program. And then those many thousands of people all over the world, often working part-time shifts, often at low wages, had to pull it off all day, every day – the cashier, the barista, the person who keeps the tables clean.

In one month I had a chance to travel from my home in Toronto to both Beijing and Madrid and experience the Starbucks phenomenon in three very different cultures. Although I am not as hooked as Sharon Vinderine and other Starbucks zealots, I can relate to what she sees and what she experiences. I can attest to the fact that the experience described happens around the world. The fast-food industry is famous for its ability to set out auditable rules and procedures that provide for a common experience across the globe. McDonald's, KFC, and Dunkin' Donuts are great companies. But to get the experience that Sharon describes requires more than auditable rules and procedures. It requires people who know, understand, and believe the vision of a company. It requires people who come to work every day feeling that delivering the vision makes them a better, more fulfilled, and happier person. It requires a system of management that respects the vision and values of the company.

Today Starbucks is a considerably different company. It is, if anything, an even more phenomenal global success. From its low of $9.46 after Schultz returned in 2006, the stock price in 2015 broke through $90. (In March 2015, the stock was split 2:1.) The company still has a compelling vision and still has an army of engaged partners and loyal customers. But it is also more tightly managed. Thoughtful leaders are thoughtful managers.

There are two important lessons from the inspiring story of Howard Schultz and Starbucks. One is that organizations need to be managed; humans need to be managed. There has to be a plan to follow, an organizational structure to work in, and a system for keeping track of progress. It doesn't just happen because everyone's heart is in the right place and everyone is doing their best. The second lesson is that the leader who manages does it in a particular way. In the planning stage, the emphasis has to be on the strategy and its relationship to the vision. They have to work together. If there is no feasible strategy that will realize the vision, the vision has to change. The organizing and staffing side has to include careful consideration of how people are aligned and whether the structure and processes will induce the behavior necessary to realize the vision and deliver the strategy. In the controlling stage, the leader as manager has to be concerned with the shortcomings and steering effects of quantitative reporting. The leader as controller has to ensure that people keep their eyes on the right ball and are motivated to do the right things.

In the next chapter we will look more closely at the leader providing direction and motivation. But we will not lose sight of the fact that direction and management work together.

Chapter Five

LEADERS PROVIDE DIRECTION

If you want to build a ship, don't drum up people to collect wood and don't assign tasks and work, but rather teach them to long for the endless immensity of the sea.

Antoine de Saint-Exupéry

Leadership is the set of actions and activities that brings people together to work for a common cause or toward a common goal. Often, when leadership is discussed and dissected, the focus is on the person who embodies the cause or articulates the goal. When I ask my students to describe a leader, they have no trouble coming up with a list of descriptors. Invariably the list can be divided into two sets of characteristics: the strong words and the soft words.

The strong words cluster around one of the dominant images of leadership, images that have to do with power: institutional power or personal power or both. The president of the United States is called "The Leader of the Free World." Jack Welch was a legendary business leader as chairman and chief executive of General Electric when it was one of the largest and most dynamic companies in the world. That same epithet is accorded to Jeff Inmelt, the man who succeeded Jack. There is still considerable focus on the late Steve Jobs for his leadership at Apple. And, of course, the previous chapter dwelled on the leadership of Howard Schultz at Starbucks. When people see this image of leadership they use words like confident, intelligent, strategic, assertive, knowledgeable, logical, organized, and even charismatic. Often when I hear these words I think what people are really saying is that they want those who have positions of power and influence to embody these characteristics. The unspoken message is that if these people are going to use the power of position, we hope that they will use it properly.

The soft words cluster around another image of leadership, images that have to do with personal influence rather than institutional power and position. Think about the famous ringing words of Dr. Martin Luther King, standing on the steps of the Lincoln Memorial, about his dream that one day his children would be judged by the content of their character and not by the color of their skin. When I ask my students who they think of as great leaders, someone will inevitably bring up Mahatma Gandhi, who led India to independence from the colonial rule of Great Britain and, through that, influenced the end of the colonial period throughout the world. When asked about my own favorite leader, I don't hesitate: Nelson Mandela. In the years between his release from prison in 1992 and his election as president in 1995, a period when he did not have titular power, he successfully led South Africa from the brink of violent revenge to a period of reconciliation and nation building. He articulated the vision of South Africa as a flock of flamingos who all rise up together, though not from the same base and not at the same pace. This image might not be as powerful to those who have never seen a flock of flamingos take flight, but the people of South Africa understood it. When people have these images of leadership, they use words like communicator, empathetic, visionary, persuasive, patient, motivator, and, yes, even charismatic.

These are the dominant images: leader as powerful person, leader as empathetic persuader. They are images that have launched a few thousand books in fiction, biography, and theory. But are they useful? What is a thoughtful person to think if they have the desire to lead some positive change but are not in a position of power and influence? What is a thoughtful person to think if they do not believe that they have been blessed with the gift of visionary persuasiveness? Can ordinary people use their "thinking slow" powers to become a leader with the tools, the skills, and the attributes they have and those they can reasonably develop?

On November 9, 1989, a group of young people began gathering at a gate on the eastern side of the famous wall separating East and West Berlin – the most dramatic symbol of the Cold War and the enforced separation of East and West Germany. They gathered all day and into the night, demanding passes through the guarded gate. On the western side another group of young people began to gather, shouting and singing songs of encouragement. The border guards kept asking for orders. A few weeks earlier they would have begun arresting or shooting. No one was prepared to give that order, but no one was prepared to open the gate. And no one wanted to shoot.

At one point, a single brave young man decided to take the initiative and just go through the gate without authorization. No shots rang out. A few more joined him. In minutes a flood of young people had passed through the gates to be greeted with flowers and champagne by the West Berliners. By midnight people had climbed the wall all along its length. In the early-morning hours someone showed up with a sledgehammer, and people started to knock the wall down. By June, only six months later, the authorities had what was left of the wall removed.

People Follow an Idea

Since leadership is about bringing a group of people together around a common cause, either we should be able to find the powerful and influential person who directed the people of Berlin to take down the wall, or we should be able to find the persuasive communicator who inspired them to commit this brave, but at the time criminal, act. In all the images and stories of that night at the Berlin Wall we can find neither. There wasn't a person directing the action. There were lots of people yelling and encouraging, but no one stands out as *the* leader. The people were inspired by an idea – a city without a wall, a united Germany, a world not divided by a Cold War. The people themselves took the action to execute that idea.

The theme I find in all great social movements is that people follow an idea. They follow an idea associated with a set of values. It's the power of the idea that gets them out on the street. It is the power of an idea that many feel but may not be able to articulate that keeps them there and keeps them united – though they do not know each other and may have no other relationship. The media tries to find a person. But the power is not in a person. It is in an idea.

Consciously or not, people who have the instinct and the ability to lead sense this need and find a way to articulate an idea that people are willing to follow. As a person articulates the idea and the values that attach to it, and gains followers, that person is given the label "leader." And they are not mislabeled. This is precisely what leaders do. In times of need, in times of crisis, even in the monotony of the day-to-day, the people whom we identify as leaders articulate the ideas that people rally behind. But it is worth pausing to reflect on the fact that the people are following the idea, not the person, or perhaps one can say that the people are following an idea personified in the individual.

Anne Mulcahy of Xerox

In May 2000, Anne Mulcahy became president and COO of Xerox. This once-mighty company was in desperate shape. It was losing money and running out of cash. It was under investigation from the SEC for accounting irregularities. It was losing market share and customers. Close observers talked of bankruptcy. As Mulcahy went on her listening tour of the company, she expected to find that people were looking for the turnaround strategy. She expected people to be looking for someone to tell them the plan for getting out of their deep, dark hole. She expected to have to exude confidence that a turnaround was possible. Instead she found that what people really wanted was the picture of what Xerox could be *when* it was turned around. People needed to know that the pain of a turnaround would be worth it when it was all over. They needed to have the dream, the idea, the vision of a better future. The turnaround itself was just mechanics.

Some people have the gift of being able to express that idea in a few simple and memorable words or lines. Some have the gift of oratory to express the idea. Winston Churchill had that gift, bringing hope to people in the United Kingdom during the darkest days of the Second World War. Dr. King galvanized a nation and much of the world with his dream of a nation where his four children would be judged by the content of their character, not the color of their skin. Barack Obama has that gift. He won the 2008 US presidential election with a vision of hope: "Yes We Can."

Few have this oratorical gift. Anne Mulcahy found a different way. She created a fictitious *Wall Street Journal* article dated five years out. In the article she described the Xerox she imagined. She gave Xerox's people an idea of where it was all going and inspired them with her vision of why the journey would be worth it. As she reports it, when the people had the idea that it would be worth it, they were able to get to work and do all the painful and difficult work of turning the business around.

However it is done – with soaring oratory, a story of the future, a compelling vision – the principle is clear. People follow an idea. The leader who can articulate, own, and personify the pursuit of a compelling idea has the power to induce people to make up their own minds and follow a new direction with purpose and passion and resolve. Leadership simply does not exist without an idea.

Kotter on Leadership

In 1990, John Kotter wrote a famous article, published in the *Harvard Business Review*: "What Do Leaders Really Do?" The article was intended to explain why so many "well-managed" companies had failed in the 1980s and why others had thrived. He believed that managing and all the disciplines associated with it were just not sufficient to cope with a world where rapid change was the norm, where opportunity could arise anywhere and at any time, and where competitive challenges were unpredictable. In such a world, the management skills of constructing a plan of action, handing out job descriptions, and standing

Figure 5.1. Kotter's leading system

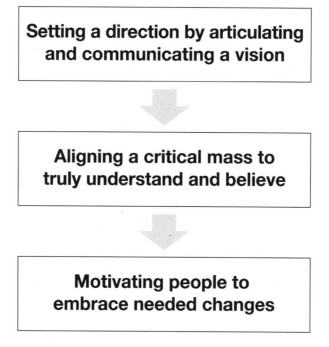

back to control the action was, in his view, unlikely to be sufficient for the task. Plans can never be good enough or durable enough to withstand the unanticipated changes that are a part of an unpredictable world. The stable conditions of the middle of the last century had produced the idea that management could be a science where everyone follows a job description. Those conditions just don't exist in many places anymore. Globalization, technological advances, and shifting demographics have made our world more exciting, more dynamic, far more prosperous, and infinitely more unpredictable. In such a world, more than ever before, enterprises need executives who can do more than manage. Kotter called this extra dimension *leadership*.

Kotter defined leadership around three elements, which can be summarized as vision, alignment, and motivation. This was an important contribution as it made a clear distinction between what he labeled leading and what had been labeled managing: plan, organize, and control. It was also critical to our thinking about leadership because it positioned leadership as work – not simply exercising authority or conjuring up some kind of charismatic magic. The words he used were deceptively simple. It is far easier to say "articulate a vision" than it is to actually come up with a vision and find the words to express it. It is far easier to accept the idea that people have to be aligned than it is to come up with approaches and strategies that achieve the alignment of enough people to make a difference. And, of course, the whole subject of human motivation is one with many nuances and challenges.

Leading as defined by Kotter is work – hard, thoughtful work. Leading as defined by Kotter could be the hardest work that anyone can undertake. Perhaps Kotter's greatest contribution was to see leadership as about something other than personal characteristics or tricks of persuasion or influence. He saw leadership as being what leaders actually do, rather than who they are or what title they might have or what tricks of influence they employ. The three elements he identified – setting a direction, aligning the organization, and motivating people to action – require hard, thoughtful work. They are not accomplished simply by giving orders. They are not accomplished through rousing speeches or powerful communication. Both of these techniques can be helpful but they will seldom or never be sufficient.

My own view is that the elements Kotter identified and labeled as leadership are an important part of leadership but not the whole story. In the previous chapter I set out how the leader as manager makes a huge difference. In the next chapter I will set out how the leader as energizer makes a huge difference. And, of course, the theme of the book is that leadership is about all three elements: *managing* so that specific jobs get accomplished; *directing* so that the purpose of the work is clear and so that people are aligned and motivated to do it; and *engaging* so that the work is done with initiative and energy. For me, Kotter's framework is an excellent model of how a leader provides direction – just one element of leadership.

The Role of a Vision

In a world of change, organizations need a compass. As they are battered by unpredictable winds, people need to have a sense of what the organization is trying to accomplish in a larger sense than the day-to-day or even the year-to-year – even if, or perhaps especially if, the carefully articulated plans become less relevant. Leaders take on the personal responsibility of crafting and then articulating that direction in the form of a vision to give context to the accompanying strategies. Vision gives purpose. A vision articulates the direction an enterprise wants to take over the longer term and broadly sets out the path it intends to follow to get there. A vision speaks to the needs and aspirations of the enterprise's key stakeholders: shareholders, employees, customers, and key suppliers. A good vision is an idea that people can accept and rally around.

As illustrated in the stories at the beginning of this chapter, there is no one way to articulate that vision. In fact, there is no one way to develop the vision. My students often ask how to go about creating a compelling vision. Although there are "how-to" manuals, in my own experience and my own research, I have found that there are many ways to get there, and there is no such thing as *the right way*.

In a famous Harvard Business School case, Rosabeth Moss Kanter tells of the long and winding journey that Charlotte Beers took at Ogilvy & Mather to create a compelling vision of "an agency most valued by companies that value brands." Beers started by finding a group of talented but restless people throughout the organization, a group "thirsty for change." She spent months on the road talking to clients, investors, and Ogilvy & Mather people. An idea was formed through several offsite brainstorming sessions. The idea was presented, adapted, and eventually adopted by the senior executive group from around the world. That idea became their vision.

Anita Roddick in *Body and Soul* – the story of the creation of the Body Shop – describes an even more inclusive process of reaching out to all employees around the world in a long, interactive process of trial and re-trial until a rough consensus was reached. The business itself, the Body Shop, is dedicated to the pursuit of social and environmental change.

The stores and products are used to help communicate human rights and environmental issues. And as for the products, "There is only one way to beautify, nature's way."

Bill George recalls becoming CEO of Medtronic and finding a wonderful company that seemed to have lost its compass. He looked up an old statement of purpose and restated it in a shortened version: Extend life; alleviate pain; reduce suffering.

One does not have to look far to find the compass for Johnson & Johnson, one of the great vision-led companies of our time. Its vision and values were written out a generation ago by the founding family: to assist health care providers to improve the lives of patients.

Or one can look at the work of A.G. Lafley as set out in *The Game-Changer*. He believed that P&G had lost its way and was too consumed with internal battles to operate as a cohesive company. Shortly after taking over, he set out a new vision for P&G (though one he believes resonated with its long and proud history): "to improve the lives of ordinary people in small but meaningful ways." That became P&G's vision statement and remains so today.

The vision idea is not just something that happens at the top. Consider this story from the trenches.

Amy's Story

A young woman (we'll call her Amy) working in the food-service business gets a job as manager of food operations for a large rehabilitation hospital. One of the characteristics of rehab facilities is that people are often there for very long stays while they receive enough treatment to get back to their home. Another characteristic is that they spend a lot of time doing very little while waiting for their daily treatments. The daily meals are a big part of the day. The three daily meals may be the only break in the monotony of waiting. In this hospital, like many others, the kitchen is in the basement, and the meals are delivered in trays on a cart to the various wards. For budgetary and logistical reasons, there are limits to what can be put into the meals and limits to how hot or cold the meal may be when it is delivered. The primary focus is on the nutritional content and its relationship to the treatment needs of the patient.

When Amy took this job, she found a very unhappy staff: high turnover, grievances, and absenteeism. These were accompanied by endless complaints from patients and their families about the quality of the meals: cold, bland, repetitive. Amy set to work.

She found out that her people were actually of vital importance to the treatment of patients. Not only was the nutrition critical, but the visit from the person delivering and picking up the trays was a welcome break for patients. And in rehab medicine, the morale of the patient can be the difference between a quick return home and a long stay in institutional rehabilitation followed by a shortened life. But her people felt so badly about what they considered the poor meals they were delivering that they got in and out of the patients' rooms as quickly as possible.

Over the next few months, Amy scheduled regular sessions for her staff with the hospital's nutritionists so that her staff could learn why the meals were put together the way they were. She scheduled sessions with the hospital's psychologists so that the staff would know how much their daily encounters could mean to patients. She arranged hospital tours for her staff so they could see what the patients actually did when they were not in their rooms. And then, working with Amy, her staff developed a vision for the department: "Five Star Nutrition … delivered with a smile." This is a story with the happiest of endings: a happy staff and contented patients, because the staff were now more likely to linger in a patient's room, even taking the time to explain the nutritional content of the meal.

This story clearly illustrates the power of a vision that speaks to the needs of the various constituents in any operation. But it also is a great illustration of all the elements that come into play when a really good vision is created.

Four Elements of a Good Vision

The first element of a well-crafted vision is that it gives meaning to the work. We all spend a huge amount of our lives at work. It would be nice if we felt that the time was meaningful in some way that we value. If the job is delivering and picking up trays, then there is not much meaning; the job becomes something that you just do and your preoccupation might become figuring out how to do the least amount of work possible – extending vacations, taking every sick day and personal day possible, and filing a grievance whenever there is an opportunity. If the job is helping people heal by delivering nutrition and a welcome, friendly interaction, then it is an entirely different situation. You might want to be there when someone is discharged. You might look forward to seeing people and observing their progress. You might become less focused on how to get the most by doing the least, because the least does not give personal satisfaction.

The second element of a vision is that it is grounded in the reality of the work to be performed. The meals will be what the nutritionists prescribe, not what the staff may want to deliver. The staff needs to know why the meal is what it is, but they are not going to be able to change it or improve it or add home cooking or whatever else might make them feel better about it. The staff can, however, deliver it with a smile and a friendly attitude as a way to contribute to patient care. The staff can go through each element of the meal and explain why its nutritional content is important. Those are contributions that the staff actually can perform. The vision does not single them out as the ones that will make the patient better, or improve their morale, or shorten their stay. Multiple factors are at play in any of those desirable outcomes. It does recognize that each individual can contribute to a positive outcome by doing what they can do – deliver a meal with a smile.

The third element is that the leader did not just appear and announce "the new vision." It was grounded in many ways. It came from her interaction with the staff to get at the root of their unhappiness. It came from a process of involving them in matters that the professional staff would assume were beyond the scope of unskilled kitchen staff – nutrition, psychology of healing – which made them feel useful and important. And then it was put into words that the staff could own.

The final element to note is that the vision worked! In the end that is the test. The vision led to behaviors that reduced grievances, absenteeism, and turnover. Those behavior changes, in turn, made the system more efficient. Lower turnover and absenteeism leads to lower cost for overtime, recruitment, and training. Having fewer grievances leads to a reduced burden on human resource and professional staffs and the consequent opportunity to focus on more productive matters. Visions are pragmatic and utilitarian. They have a job to do and should be assessed against their utility in doing that job.

A Pragmatic and Utilitarian Vision

The point of all these stories is to illustrate that visions perform a function. Leaders recognize that function and understand that it cannot be ignored. Through one mechanism or another, leaders create that compelling idea – more powerful than profit, share price, total shareholder return, or any external metric – around which people can rally. Vision is what induces people to say to themselves, "This is what I come to work to accomplish." Vision fills that essential task of making work meaningful. And because the vision has such a vital impact, it is so important that leaders get it right. It has to be attached to a winning strategy, with all the hard work and thought implied in that simple statement. It has to speak to the various constituents that need to be led. In the case of a company, this will include workers, investors, customers, suppliers, and often many more groups. In the case of a unit, it will include the people in the unit but also senior leadership – the bosses, peer units, and the groups being served, as well as those who provide support.

Communicate the Vision

Leaders do more than ensure that an appropriate vision is crafted. They see it as their responsibility to articulate and communicate that vision. The old image of the leader as the one with the vision who keeps it to herself or to a close group of confidantes, doling it out with just the right instructions to the workers to make it happen, is an old and outdated image. Today, leaders must engage the minds and energies of everyone in the enterprise. That means that everyone needs to know the organization's purpose. The leader and the leadership group have to be the articulators and communicators of the enterprise's vision – the custodian of its essential purpose. That custodial job can become mistaken for the idea that people follow the leader. That is an important mistake for the putative leader to avoid. The leader should always remember that it is the idea they embody that people are following. The communication has to focus on the idea, not the person. It is not "follow me." It is, rather, "let's go here together."

It starts with a *vision*. In the next chapter we will get into some of the things that bring a vision to life, but it has to start with a vision, a dream of what we might become if we stay together and work together and give it our best. The vision has to be understood at a visceral, emotional level as well as at a substantive and logical level. People need a deep understanding so that they can sense what actions and initiatives need to be taken when there is no one there to answer their questions. People need to be *aligned*. The subtle and not-so-subtle messages of an organization must be aligned.

Gain Alignment

Communication too often implies a one-way monologue of orchestrated speeches and posters. Alignment is something more. Leaders are to ensure that there is at least a critical mass of people who are truly aligned with the vision. *Alignment* means that they understand the roots of the vision, where it came from, and the critical issues that were considered. They need to understand it and believe it. Jack Welch, the iconic CEO of General Electric, can be heard saying, way back in 1987 to a class at the Harvard Business School, "that is why me and my leadership group never pass up the opportunity of *selling* our vision." Selling is a powerful word. It implies that the listener is an active, not a passive, player in the dialogue. It implies that the leader must truly convince the listener that the vision is right and appropriate for the situation. If the listener does not buy the vision, the job is not done. In fact, it was always Jack Welch's dream that GE people would be smart, tough, and independent; he wanted people who had to be sold. He didn't want obedience; he wanted commitment.

When a vision is both feasible and desirable, then alignment becomes empowering. When people really know, understand, and agree with the enterprise's direction, they can take initiatives that are more likely to be appropriate. And for most enterprises, it is those thousands of small initiatives taken by people on their own, without asking for permission, unknown and unheeded by senior executives, which make all the difference. As Colin Powell, former Chief of Staff and Secretary of Defense in the United States, has said, the only ones who know how the war is going are the soldiers at the front. The generals are just guessing. The soldiers at the front need to truly and deeply understand and commit to the mission for it to be a success.

One of the reasons a leader has to think hard about alignment is that people who have to be aligned are seldom just the team that seems most directly involved. Everything happens within some kind of community of interdependence. An assignment comes from somewhere and the output will serve another group. Timelines and resource allocations come from someone in a position of power and influence. Peers can often make or break an initiative. Looking even further afield, consider an organization building in a municipality, needing building permits and licenses to operate. That wider constituency can make the job easier or more difficult. Leaders get things done. And often, perhaps usually, that means leading, achieving real alignment beyond the immediate team.

Motivate

How do we get the front line to take the right initiatives? How do we get support groups to support? Communicating the vision and getting people aligned is necessary but not sufficient. We all know that there is within us reluctance, even resistance, to change. Change requires energy. Taking an initiative requires courage. Doing something different will always be uncertain. People have to be motivated. They have to be prepared to enter the discomfort zone, to take a risk. Leaders recognize the need for motivation and work at creating it. Reward systems that recognize movement toward the vision and that appeal to pride, to the opportunity to make a difference and to be part of something bigger than oneself – these are the things that drive the motivation that turns vision and alignment into action.

For people to get over the line, to actually take action, to change comfortable patterns, to take a risk, to put the vision before their own personal needs, they have to be *motivated*. They have to feel that trying to achieve the vision is worth it. There are, of course, many ways to motivate. Frederick Herzberg years ago set out a useful framework of extrinsic and intrinsic motivation. The extrinsic includes money, status, perks, and benefits. Herzberg believed people become dissatisfied if the extrinsic factors seem unfair. But getting the extrinsic elements right does not lead directly to job satisfaction or to a highly motivated worker. Deep satisfaction come from the intrinsic: making a difference; making the world a little better; developing and using one's personal skills; becoming a better person; working with good people; becoming valued by people whom we value. Over the decades the power and interplay of these two sources of motivation have been studied and written about by countless academics.

Extrinsic motivation is often seen as the purview of the economists. Much of economics is based on the premise that people respond to incentives. Offering rewards for performance is, then, a common-sense way to motivate. It is relatively easy to see the extrinsic motivators. Professionals are often compensated on pay-for-service systems. Bonus programs are common in corporations and often advocated as a way to improve performance in public systems. Teachers are offered incentives to continue their education through formulas that take them to higher pay levels as they complete additional courses. Beyond money, other common applications of the extrinsic motivation idea are found in award programs, higher status titles, office allocations, and the like. In the academic literature there is debate about whether these extrinsic motivators are helpful or harmful. Whatever stand one takes on that debate, it is important to note that the extrinsic motivators are easily replicated by other organizations. If people are only there for the money, they are easily lured to another place that offers a little more or an extra perk. And if they are only there for the extrinsic motivators, they are easily corrupted into spending their time thinking about how to game the situation: getting low targets for bonus eligibility; cutting off sales early if targets are already met; and many, many other practices common in workplaces where the extrinsic factors are the main motivational tools.

Visions speak primarily to the intrinsic. People who are truly aligned with the vision are not so easily corrupted. People who believe in the vision, who identify with its underlying idea, become motivated by the intrinsic factors. They are more likely to set challenging goals because they believe in the mission. They are less likely to move sales into next year if they believe that they are selling a product or service that really makes a difference or if they believe that the strength of the enterprise is important to them individually. They are more likely to work hard on a project that does not directly lead to monetary payoff if they believe that it is furthering the progress of an enterprise in which they believe.

The leader who can build a foundation of intrinsic motivation in the workplace on the articulated vision, the big idea, has the greatest chance of succeeding. The person who can articulate and sell that sense of purpose will create followers who will do their best – and who can realistically ask for more.

Directing

These concepts can be incorporated into what I call *Directing*, incorporating the idea of developing and articulating a vision, taking the steps necessary to create alignment with the vision, and working on all the elements that motivate commitment to the vision. In the chart in Figure 5.2 I have set the Directing ideas beside the Managing ideas because they are so closely linked. The vision has to come out of, or find life in, a winning strategy and then be turned into action through a plan. Organizational arrangements of all kinds, from hiring to job descriptions to working processes, are intended to align people with the work to be done, which has been expressed in the vision and plans. And when

Figure 5.2. Managing and Directing: two of the cornerstones of effective leadership

MANAGING	DIRECTING
PLAN • Finding a winning strategy • Setting targets and goals • Allocating resources against the strategy	**VISION** • Setting a direction—developing a workable vision for the future • Articulating the vision in clear language
ORGANIZE • Designing an organization that focuses on the strategic imperatives • Assembling and developing the team • Monitoring and adjusting the organization to deal with changing circumstances	**ALIGNMENT** • Identifying the various constituencies that have to be led • Communicating the vision in a way that is understood and relevant • Selling the vision to ensure commitment
CONTROL • Monitoring results and reports to ensure goals are being met • Paying attention to dysfunctional steering effects from the controls as designed • Devising ways to assess the commitment of the organization to the vision	**MOTIVATION** • Appealing to the basic but often untapped human needs, values, and emotions • Stirring a sense of belonging and self-esteem in the fulfillment of the vision • Ensuring people see the personal payoff from achieving the vision

people are motivated to achieve some worthwhile end, they will want to know if progress is being made, which ties directly to the control side of managing.

The next chapter will look at how leaders get deep engagement by building a culture that creates a team where everyone is always looking for ways to do better.

Chapter Six

CREATE ENERGY THROUGH ENGAGEMENT

But of a good leader, who talks little, when his work is done, his aims fulfilled, they will all say, "We did this ourselves."

Lao Tzu

Linda Hasenfratz, CEO of Linamar Corporation, inspects a car-parts plant.

> Her bright blue eyes, encased behind safety goggles, rove constantly. Is there excess inventory kicking around? How many machines are up? Is the place a mess, or are the workers adhering to the "5S" organizational system: sort, set in order, shine, standardize and sustain? A tidy workplace, she says, is an efficient one.
>
> She likes what she sees. All lines are running, which means orders are picking up. Every tool is hung in its proper place. Most important of all, though, are the smiles. "If I walk through a plant and no one wants to look me in the eyes," she says, "I know I've got a problem in there."

How the world has changed! It is said that when Henry Ford roamed his plants, anyone seen smiling was fired on the spot. Head down, serious work was the order of the day. And I can clearly recall sitting in a training session at a major chartered bank – my first job after graduating from university – being told that if as we performed various clerical functions we saw a better way to do them, we should keep it to ourselves. "If there was a better way, people with experience would have already found it."

The time between those three stories – Henry Ford, my job as a bank trainer, and Linda Hasenfranz – is not that long, but what a distance has been traveled: from work is serious, keep your head down, and do as you are told; to simply do as you are told and be happy about it; to look up, smile, and get involved. In the 1980s the Japanese automakers took Europe and North America by storm with their high-quality, afford-able, mass-market cars. Their system of high productivity through high levels of disciplined worker involvement was so obviously superior to the prevailing view of engineer-led, top-down production disciplines that even the most thorough skeptic had to pay attention. And yet, in the 1990s, when I was responsible for a large North American bakery business that was not subject to competitive pressures from the great global manufacturers, there was still no acceptance of these ideas. Two stories illustrate how far we had to travel.

Story One: The Perfect Plant

Production people dream about what they call a "lights out" operation. By this they mean a plant that does not need any lighting because there are no people. In this idealized world, the plant starts up and operates on its own – entirely automated, zero labor cost, no one to mess up the machines, no grievances, no coffee breaks. In 1990 we opened a plant that was as close to that ideal as any bakery we knew about in the world. On Sunday night, with only a few security people on the prem-ises, the flour silo would open to drop 2,000 pounds of flour into a mixer. Water, yeast, and the rest of the ingredients would be added au-tomatically and the mixer would start to churn. At just the right time, the mixer would stop and drop the dough into a giant container, which would move on tracks into a temperature- and humidity-controlled space to rise. Sometime early the next morning, a worker would show up to check the dough before it went through the next steps of proofing, forming, baking, cooling, slicing, packaging, and loading onto trays to be sent to the shippers in the distribution area. Twelve thousand perfect loaves an hour with only a few workers to monitor the operation. Monitor but don't touch! A dream operation.

But our dream was a nightmare. The "dream" claimed the careers of several plant managers. Too often something went wrong. The temperature or humidity would not reach the right level at the right moment. The exact quantity of a critical ingredient would not make it into the mix at precisely the right time. A pump would have surges, operating too fast and then too slow. Temperature gradients throughout the oven would be inconsistent. It was infuriatingly unpredictable – sometimes perfect, often not, but seldom the same problem twice. The job of getting fresh product into the market every day was a constant scramble, with many "workarounds." It was a constant financial drain and a frequently reported "excuse" for our disappointing results.

And so it continued until we sent yet another plant manager into the fray. The plant and technology was new to him, so he did something that his predecessors had not done. He decided to ask the workers. Over many beers at the end of numerous shifts, the workers (many of whom were functionally illiterate) drew on paper napkins, still wet from the last round, a picture of how the machines actually operated – not how they were supposed to operate. Together with the plant manager they gradually got at the many small but consequential problems. In a few months the plant was operating as it was intended. In a few more months it began operating at speeds that were even higher than the engineers had designed, with continuing excellent quality. Shipping every day became a routine operation.

I should tell you one more thing. The plant was in the Province of Quebec and the workers were unilingual Francophone. The plant manager was unilingual Anglophone.

Story Two: Delivering the Bread

Perhaps the most critical job in a bakery is getting the product to the shelf. The commercial bakery business is a classic high-volume, low-margin business. The product itself is perishable, damages easily, and occupies a considerable volume for its value. When the consumer goes out to buy bread, the expectation is that the shelf will be well stocked and neatly displayed. Normally retailers turn this chore over to their commercial bakery supplier. Very early every morning, across the continent, thousands of trucks are loaded with the production of the previous day and night. Drivers take the product to the stores, straighten the shelves, rotate the stock, add fresh product and look for attractive ways to display the product. Volumes vary by day. The type of product varies with the seasons, the weather, and the neighborhood served by the store.

The system that I inherited operated much the same as other North American bakeries. The drivers were paid a salary and commission – recognizing the routine aspect of the job as well as the value added that would come from service and merchandising. Since every store and every shelf was different, a key to growing sales and profitability was to get the right product onto the right shelf every day of every season. Our entire system was unionized, with many rules established over many rounds of collective bargaining. The industry was competitive enough that the rules and procedures were generally sensible and productive. The operation was organized into areas and regions under the guidance of route supervisors and regional managers. The supervisors had the front-line job of dealing with customers, monitoring service quality, handling vacation and absenteeism replacement issues, and keeping on top of the ordering system to ensure that appropriate product was on the truck each day. At the end of every day, the drivers would return to the depot to unload returned product and reconcile the balance delivered with the invoices that would be sent to our customers. It was a busy system, carried out in all kinds of weather in all seasons, coping with new customers and lost customers, new products and discontinued products. There was a lot of detail. Everyone was busy.

There was something about the system that always bothered me. For one thing, although we called the first level of management "supervisors," it was clear that there was not much supervising going on. It was not the fault of the supervisors. It was simply the fact of the job. Trucks were all over the place from very early in the morning. City traffic made it difficult to get to many stops to check up on the drivers, so there was not much monitoring going on. The additions and cuts of products and customers, training new people and scheduling vacation replacements, filling in on a route when someone called in sick, and attending management meetings kept supervisors busy for what was often a very long day. In the end, I observed that the route drivers were not supervised. They were operating on their own. When I rode along with drivers, I was always struck by how much they enjoyed this very aspect of their job. They were, for all practical purposes, their own bosses. Their social contact was with their customers – not the managers of their customers but the people like them who do the work to keep things going. And their friends on the road were the other drivers who were supposed to be their competitors. They didn't really compete; they took care of each other.

I became convinced that the better way to operate a route delivery system was to recognize the independence of the drivers and make them owner-operators with responsibility for servicing a geographical area with clear financial parameters. This idea was not well received. I was the college boy with no experience in the industry who had a theoretical solution to a problem no one thought existed. I was the MBA who was only interested in the short-term numbers – the gain we would realize if we sold the routes to the drivers. And the anecdotal information was that only bakeries in their last dying days sold their routes. It was a sign that the end was near. There wasn't really a way to "try it out." One of our operations had to make a commitment and go for it or it would never happen.

As it turned out, one of our operations did run into trouble with its distribution system and, as a last resort, was forced to try the owner-operator approach. An inspired management team did a magnificent job of implementing the transition. They started by "optimizing" the routes, ensuring that the sales per route were as close to potential as they could manage. Then they worked out a price for each route so a driver could buy the route and the truck to service it, financed in such a way that if volumes were maintained, their take-home pay would continue as before. Almost every driver accepted the deal.

The new system turned out to be better than anyone imagined. Several drivers bought their route, doubled their volume in a few months, sold half to get their investment back, doubled the half that they kept, and sold that as well. Customers were delighted with the service and merchandising they were experiencing. All of a sudden our trucks were cleaner and shinier than they had ever been. Instead of struggling to get the trucks in for washing, we were struggling to keep up with the demands for better cleaning facilities. Drivers invented ways of operating their routes that we had not imagined. The whole family could get involved, with one spouse handling the deliveries and the other the merchandising. It was amazing. People were telling me that of course this was the way they had always thought things should be done. It was hard not to crow.

It's Not Enough Simply to Do What You're Told

It is hard to tell stories like that and not dwell on the brilliance of the leadership that inspired them. But that would miss the point. The real point is that the collective brilliance was within the front-line workers. All management had to do was find a way to bring them into the game. The stories are also from a very old and very traditional industry – an industry characterized by a single-minded pursuit of efficiency, consistency, and repetition. It is not an industry that is challenged by globalization or rapid adoption of new technology. It is not the kind of industry we normally think of as one that calls out for creativity and innovation. And yet it still exemplifies the idea that much can be accomplished if you can tap into the collective intelligence of everyone in the workplace. Richard Florida has made famous the idea that all work today is creative work. My observation is that all work has always had within it the opportunity to be treated as creative work, with the resultant gains reaped. And once that idea is accepted, I don't know if there are any jobs or enterprises that will survive by having a workforce that just does what it is told.

In the previous chapter I set out the benefits of giving a group, a team, or a workforce direction: a deeper understanding of why the work should be done. When people understand the mission and are aligned with it, they can be motivated to do the work well. But it seems that today we need something more. Today, we need a truly engaged work-force, a workforce that Herzberg would recognize as one that finds real satisfaction in the intrinsic rewards of seeing work as an opportunity to grow, contribute, and feel good about one's personal growth.

How does a leader act, knowing that the key to real success is to be able to truly engage the workforce? It certainly takes more than management, though all work has to be managed. And it takes more than direction setting, though direction is essential to motivate focused action. It takes something that I call engagement, but readers of contemporary leadership literature will recognize it as that bundle of elements that induce people to really put their hearts into the work. Engagement is what keeps the teacher who volunteers to lead the debating team at work far after peers have gone home. It is engagement that brings the nurse back to check up on a patient after the shift is over. Engagement brings out the extra effort and commitment that can make the critical difference between doing a job and doing a job well.

Engagement is a tricky topic for a leader. The skills of management can be learned and practiced. Deviations can be seen and corrected. Direction setting is more of an art form but it is, or can be, a cerebral activity. Visions connected to strategy can be crafted with help. Alignment is often a product of thoughtful, well-drafted, and persistent communication. Motivation is more complex but, at the very least, levels of motivation can be assessed and corrective action taken. Engagement is more difficult, both to create and to assess. It takes a lot of thought and care. It won't be found in a binder or tacked up on a wall beside the vision statement. It is about creating a culture where people care about their work, about each other, about their customer, and about how all that affects their relationship to their community. It is not easy to assess how engaged an organization or group really is. And it is really difficult to achieve. The Gallup poll showing that only 30 percent of American workers are engaged in their work is testimony to how difficult it is.

I struggled to find a framework that is up to such a challenging assignment. I have found pieces that are helpful: something about being authentic, something about integrity and transparency, something about trusting relationships, something about being the servant leader.

These are all interesting ideas, but a thoughtful leader needs a way to make sense of them holistically. The best approach I have found came from *Leadership and the Quest for Integrity* by Joseph Badaracco and Richard Ellsworth.

The Badaracco and Ellsworth Framework

In *Leadership and the Quest of Integrity*, Badaracco and Ellsworth surveyed what is known about motivation to provide a way for leaders to think about how to act consistently. I have found it to be a useful and usable way for a leader to think about how their actions can create an engaged workforce, though I have made a few modifications. They suggest that leaders can use one of three leadership approaches.

Values-Driven Leadership reaches into what motivates people to perform over long periods of time in all kinds of conditions. It reaches into how one creates a culture in an organization – a set of unwritten but powerful rules about how to behave when no one is looking. In a sense it is more about institution building than simply about achieving immediate results. It continues the journey into the understanding of how people seek meaning at work by going deeper into what makes people feel good about themselves. The belief is that people will only truly commit to an enterprise that lives up to a set of values and engages them at a very fundamental level. Working for such an organization makes people feel better about themselves. They become more engaged workers and better citizens, parents, and partners.

But values leadership is about more than having people feel better about themselves. The work has to get done. The values-driven leader believes that if the values of an organization are properly shaped, people will see the problems and opportunities and tackle them in appropriate ways. They don't have to be told. Note that values-driven leadership is pragmatic, not absolute. It does not advocate one kind of "golden rule" or "Judeo-Christian ethic" or universal belief about good behavior. The values could be extremist. They could be competitive. They could be collaborative. They could be good. They could be evil. Good and evil are often in the eye of the beholder. What they do

Figure 6.1. Three approaches to leadership

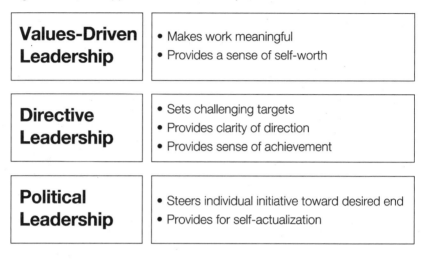

Values-Driven Leadership	• Makes work meaningful • Provides a sense of self-worth
Directive Leadership	• Sets challenging targets • Provides clarity of direction • Provides sense of achievement
Political Leadership	• Steers individual initiative toward desired end • Provides for self-actualization

is provide useful guidance for behavior, engaging the group to behave that way consistently and continuously.

Directive Leadership has a different root. It recognizes that people become really engrossed in what they are doing when it is clear what has to be done, when there is a challenging goal to reach, and when feedback on progress is provided. It also recognizes that there are substantial splintering forces in any organization, especially one composed of strong people. A clear and necessary duty of any leader is to make the tough call when there is not an apparent internal consensus on a particular course of action. The directive leader does not let the organization become paralyzed by debate. The directive leader makes the timely decision before the organization becomes paralyzed or factionalized. The directive leader ensures that the organization's goals are clear, desirable, and tough, but also feasible.

Directive leadership is not, of course, ignorant or disconnected leadership. This leader does not sit back in an office removed from the action and issues directives. The directive leader is in the field, talking to people, understanding the issues, and sensing when and on what issues the enterprise needs direction. The belief is that to achieve exceptional performance, goals must be clear, specific, challenging, and compelling. There is a great deal of behavioral research that supports the idea that striving for a specific challenging goal produces better results than "doing your best." And there is considerable evidence that goals bring unity of purpose to any organization.

Political Leadership takes still a different approach. The political leader recognizes that people become engaged in their work when they feel that they have had true involvement in defining the work. Strong people don't want to be told what to do. They want to figure it out for themselves. They will work harder and smarter to implement an initiative that they originated than they would to carry out a task specified for them. At all levels of an organization, people want to feel involved in their work – not coerced into following some remote routine. This is a tricky problem for a leader. Leaders know that all followers have this need. They know that to bring out the best in people they must accede to it, but they also know they cannot allow chaos. They need to allow people to have some control over their work space, but they still need to drive the organization to the desired end.

The astute political leader will recognize that leadership is often about persuasion, about throwing out hints and suggestions, about making goals flexible enough to allow for personal interpretation, about being willing to move gradually, incrementally, and patiently to the ultimate goal. This style of leadership requires a great deal of maturity and has to be based on the fundamental belief that the end result will be better than if the leader was clearer, more direct, and more controlling.

The underlying motivation of the political leadership approach is involvement. The political leader fundamentally believes that the more people feel their work is really a part of themselves – that they identified the problems and crafted the solutions – the more committed they will be to achieving a really outstanding result. The political leader can believe that a good solution well executed is better than a great solution poorly executed, or that well-motivated people close to the action are more likely to find better solutions than the removed expert, or both. The trick is to channel that dispersed energy into a direction that takes the enterprise where it should go. The *political* in political leadership is the ability to channel without being so intrusive that people feel manipulated. One way to achieve this balance is to be clear about direction – the vision – and to have an effective management system.

An Integrated Approach to Engagement

Badaracco and Ellsworth's idea of values-based, directive, and political leadership is, in my judgment, an excellent place to start. However, where we differ is that they believe a leader needs to choose one of the approaches and have a bias toward that approach. In my experience, a leader absolutely must use all three approaches. Leadership doesn't happen any other way. There has to be a set of values that lead to consistent, predictable behavior, values that define the way the leader wants others to act. There must be clear goals and clear, strong decisions on issues that matter to the organization. And leaders absolutely need to find a way to make every single person feel that their contribution is needed and appreciated. The most effective leaders are values-based, directive, and political and are that way all the time.

Borrowing from the Badaracco and Ellsworth framework, Figure 6.2 shows a way to think about how to engage.

James MacGregor Burns wrote eloquently about transformational leaders who rise above the work of the transactional leadership in order to draw out all the energy that could be committed to work but is held back. Transformational leaders engage. The fact is that people have a great deal of control over how much effort they put into their work. People can go through the motions or perform to the best of their abilities. Perhaps nothing illustrates this better than the tactics of an angry union whose members "work to rule." It is a devastating tactic because it shows so clearly how we much rely on judgment and initiative from each and every individual. A leader who can tap into the reservoir of withheld energy will bring out the effort, creativity, and courage that only come from the really committed person. One need only look at the energy of the religious or nationalistic fanatic to see how much energy humans have within. But engagement cannot be achieved with just one action bias. It takes all three.

Figure 6.2. How to engage

ENGAGING
VALUES
• Defining the values that bring the vision to life
• Articulating the values in a way that is meaningful to everyone
• Modeling the values by living them every day
CLARITY
• Ensuring clear targets and goals are set that are consistent with the vision and strategy
• Searching for and making decisions where open problems are slowing down the organization
• Ensuring that everyone is aware of the boundaries for action
INVOLVEMENT
• Ensuring that systems and procedures are in place that allow everyone to be involved
• Holding back when necessary to allow others to find the solution
• Devising ways to assess the organization's level of involvement

Values are a critical element in persuading people to make a personal investment in the enterprise. Values once espoused must always be respected. People believe what they see more than what they hear. Values call an enterprise to a challenge that goes beyond the external metrics, whether financial returns or test scores or patient satisfaction metrics. These metrics can often be seen as the means to achieve a higher end or a signal of progress toward a higher end but are not the end itself. And there is a huge array of values to which an enterprise can aspire: about contribution to humanity; about the way people work together; about commitment to integrity and honesty in all dealings inside and outside the enterprise; about the team that never loses or about the team that never quits; about the team that never compromises on quality to make a sale or a bottom line or about a team that does what it has to do to meet a target. They can be values that we all admire or values that not everyone condones. Values-driven leaders have lots of values to choose from, but whatever the choice, values provide essential context to the vision.

I believe the most effective way for a leader to think about values is as pragmatic, not idealistic. They have a job to do. An enterprise focused on delivering a tangible product could work well with values that focus on integrity – building and delivering a product that performs as it should. A.G. Lafley of P&G made integrity a cornerstone value of that consumer goods company. An enterprise focused on delivering a service may develop a set of values that are more personal, about how people should be treated. Issy Sharp built the world's leading luxury hotel chain around the golden rule, treating everyone as you would like to be treated. A retailer like Walmart builds a set of values around doing everything possible to drive down costs in order to improve the standard of living of the people on the bottom half of the economic ladder. And of course Google built a business around "Do No Evil," a value that is essential to being a trusted search engine and which has also been critical to their ability to develop the culture that drives their phenomenal growth. There is no one right set of values. There is, however, a set of values that molds the right kind of behavior for the action the leader is trying to induce.

Clarity is an important prerequisite for meaningful engagement. Clear goals bring things into focus. Clear decisions on matters of importance end frustration and a feeling of helplessness. It is more important for a leader to understand the power of clarity than to focus on being directive as the way to get clarity. Latham and Locke wrote the seminal work on the role of targets and the power of specificity of those targets. Clear goals, even if they are challenging, often reduce stress by creating focus and reducing ambiguity. Clarity gives meaning to organizational decisions. It provides specificity to those places where the leader is trying to get alignment. Clarity is an important element of the engagement mix. When the product – clarity – is emphasized, rather than the means to clarity, it can be seen that there is no conflict with values. They work together. Values tell people how to work. Clarity tells them what to work on.

Involvement can be thought of either as the payoff for engagement or as the reason that engagement is needed. As the payoff, the leader who has engaged the group will see people taking initiative and acting when problems and opportunities arise rather than sitting back and waiting to be told what to do or simply following normal operation procedures. There is a story from Google that has become part of the mythology of the company. On a Friday afternoon, Larry Page typed a few words into the search engine to see how the entries appeared and how they were matched with appropriate advertising. He found some searches and ad matches that were not very good. Before he went home for the weekend, he printed out the poorest ones, drew a circle around the offending sections, and pinned them up on the bulletin board in the lunchroom. There were no comments or directives or exhortations. He did not put his name on the paper. When he showed up for work Monday morning, the problem had been fixed. A few people had come into the lunchroom before going home for the weekend. They agreed that the results were poor and they didn't like it. They were also intrigued by what might have caused it and how it might be fixed. They spent the weekend on it, not because they were ordered to or even asked to. They did not expect to get an exceptional bonus or other tangible reward. They simply wanted to do it. They were engaged.

The workers in the bakery "dream plant" discussed earlier saw the problems and had thought about possible solutions, but they kept their ideas to themselves. Perhaps they did not feel engaged. Perhaps they did not feel it was their place to take on the better-educated engineers, let alone the more senior bosses. And there was no vehicle for getting them involved until the new plant manager showed up and took them out for a beer. Most people will hold back until there is a very clear signal that involvement is appropriate, despite their station. And most people will hold back unless there is a clear mechanism to draw them in. Involvement has to be organized. It has to be expected and facilitated. It will seldom just happen organically.

And engagement is needed. The stories at the beginning of the chapter illustrate the power that comes from getting everyone involved. The untapped energy and initiative in front-line workers is evident in the story of the drivers' transition from employee to owner-operator of our route trucks. It was all there, if we had only been clever enough to find a way to get them engaged.

Engagement requires action in all three elements. Involvement means ensuring that there are clear opportunities for involvement, mechanisms to draw people in, and expectations that involvement is appropriate and expected. This comes directly from the values, which are either inclusive or restrictive. The values also set guidelines for what kind of action will be acceptable and what behavior is appropriate within the organization and in interactions outside the organization. Clarity makes involvement possible by giving specificity to those places where the organization needs to perform. A person working on a software project team needs to know whether the goal is getting something working quickly or getting a program that interacts with other systems. Both are important; which gets priority? And that same person needs to have a feeling for the values that underlie how the work is done. Are the values collaborative, which might mean slowing down to help someone out, or are they meritocratic, which might mean going all out to get the assignment completed? Both are possible; which is more highly valued? A front-line salesperson needs to know whether to go all in to capture a new customer or to go the extra mile to take care of an existing customer.

Figure 6.3. The complete model of integrative leadership

MANAGING	DIRECTING	ENGAGING
PLAN • Finding a winning strategy • Setting targets and goal • Allocating resources against the strategy	**VISION** • Setting a direction—developing a workable vision for the future • Articulating the vision in clear language	**VALUES** • Defining the values that bring the vision to life • Articulating the values in a way that is meaningful to everyone • Modeling the values by living them every day
ORGANIZE • Designing an organization that focuses on the strategic imperatives • Assembling and developing the team • Monitoring and adjusting the organization to deal with changing circumstances	**ALIGNMENT** • Identifying the various constituencies that have to be led • Communicating the vision in a way that is understood and relevant • Sellling the vision to ensure commitment	**CLARITY** • Ensuring clear targets and goals are set that are consistent with the vision and strategy • Searching for and making decisions where open problems are slowing down the organization • Ensuring that everyone is aware of the boundaries for action
CONTROL • Monitoring results and reports to ensure goals are being met • Paying attention to dysfunctional steering effects from the controls as designed • Devising ways to assess the commitment of the organization to the vision	**MOTIVATION** • Appealing to the basic but often untapped human needs, values, and emotions • Stirring a sense of belonging and self-esteem in the fulfillment of the vision • Ensuring people see the personal payoff from achieving the vision	**INVOLVEMENT** • Ensuring that systems and procedures are in place that allow everyone to be involved • Holding back when necessary to allow others to find the solution • Devising ways to assess the organization's level of involvement

Engagement gets at the thousands and thousands of decisions made and actions taken every day in every workplace out from under the watchful eye of those who are supposed to be in charge. But engagement also gets at the team member who might be sitting quietly in the meeting wondering whether to speak up or go along. For engagement to happen, it has to be encouraged with known, although often unwritten, rules of behavior and clarity about goals and priorities. All three elements work together.

Chapter Seven

THE DYNAMICS OF LEADERSHIP

Chapter 1 set out three models of leadership as practiced, or what leaders do to create useful followers – energized, active, initiative-seeking followers. The three accepted models of what it takes to get work done through people include a model for managing, a model for providing direction, and a model for engaging. I described each of these models vertically: from plan to organize to control; from vision to alignment to motivation; from values to clarity to involvement. As I presented and explained each idea, I drew a picture of what that model might look like to help the reader visualize the elements and their relationships. Chapter 2 showed how the three models work together – integrative at all levels.

There is always a problem in how models are described. The problem is endemic to the written word and to our visual senses. The inherent limitation of the oral or written word is that it comes to the listener or reader in a linear form: A then B then C. As the headings build, there is a sense that there is only one sequence that makes sense. The pictures I used as a visual reference stack the words from top to bottom in the same order and are read from left to right, reinforcing that same sequence. In practice, the concepts are more iterative and dynamic. Certainly one has to have some sense of a *plan* before knowing how and what to *organize*. But that plan will surely be influenced by the availability and existence of a team or an organizational competence. The familiar dictum that "what gets measured gets managed" can be looked at as indicating that results appearing in the *control* box determine what gets planned and organized. In other words, the Managing model makes as much sense from bottom to top as it does from top to bottom. One can make the same case with each of the other models.

A *vision* may seem great until one finds a critical constituency that cannot be *aligned*. In that case it is back to the drawing board to rethink the vision. Visions have to work. They have to be saleable. A leader may judge that a team or organization is just not as motivated as they once were or as much as that leader expects. That may take the leader back up the model to assess whether there is a gap in alignment or whether the vision is not doing its job. When I took on the bakery job, I was selling the vision that we had to feel in control of the business and that we were not going to be the division that always came to the annual meeting having fallen short yet again. When that was accomplished, I had to switch the vision to being the best commercial bakery in North American measured on a series of metrics. People had to believe that the new vision was possible, while acknowledging that it would take a lot of work – alignment. And people had to see how much better they would feel to be part of a bakery which was that good – motivation.

The linkages in the Engaging model are even more flexible. Each is actually an element that on its own contributes to building an energized workplace. Clarity is both a motivational tool (following the Latham and Locke theory of the power of clear, tough goals to focus and energize work) and the element that provides people an opportunity to be involved. If people don't know what is expected, they cannot be involved. They have to wait to be told what to do.

Of course, this would not be an integrated model if it did not integrate in every dimension – vertically, horizontally, and diagonally. When I developed this model I was not entirely sure that it did. In fact, in my early years using the model I assumed that one had to find a way of leading that was consistent with the implied message in each of the vertical models. An image I used was that leaders appeal to the head by providing direction, to the arms and legs by managing, and to the heart by engaging. Effective leaders do each of these things. And I could find support for this idea in well-known books related to leadership.

Dan Pink's popular and brilliantly written *Drive: The Surprising Truth About What Motivates Us* set out what he called "the Type I tripod" of autonomy, mastery, and purpose. He calls autonomy "the newfangled emphasis on self-direction." The conditions that permit and encourage self-direction are very close to what I call Engaging. The second leg of his tripod is mastery. Mastery depends on working long and hard on a particular task or skill toward an end result. Managing provides a frame for achieving mastery. The third leg is purpose. Everything motivating about purpose can be found in the elements of Directing.

Simon Sinek's wildly popular TED talk and successful book, *Start With Why: How Great Leaders Inspire Everyone to Take Action*, also relate to the three models and his contention that great leaders do all three. His "golden circle" is about starting with Why, which maps to Direction; then goes to How, which maps roughly to Engage (especially in the unwritten rules that are part of any strong values-based culture); and then goes to What, which maps to Managing. The idea that effective leaders do these three sets of things is reinforced by the wide acceptance of the work of Pink and Sinek, although there are subtle differences in the way that each of them describes the three approaches.

I could have let my thinking stop there and been content, but over time, former students kept coming back to me with stories about how they used the model. Their stories convinced me to explore the multidimensional linkages among the various components of the integrated model. It is, in fact, the connection and consistency that makes the model so powerful. And it is the need for connection and consistency that makes the model require so much thought and care. In the sections that follow I will show how it is integrated in all dimensions, starting with the horizontal rows.

The first linkage to explore is the horizontal linkage across the top. When I sat in the audience listening to the many speakers brought to the Rotman School in support of the Integrative Thinking initiative, I was struck by how many of them spoke about the elements of Plan – Vision – Values. Issy Sharp talked about his dream, which became a vision, of building the world's leading luxury hotel chain. Beyond his talk at the school, Issy's vision and quest to attain it are well documented on the

Figure 7.1. Plan – Vision – Values: horizontal linkages

MANAGING	DIRECTING	ENGAGING
PLAN	VISION	VALUES

Four Seasons website and were laid out in his book, *Four Seasons: The Story of a Business Philosophy*. He recognized very early that if he defined luxury as architecture and amenities, all his good ideas would soon be copied. Someone would build a fancier hotel and everyone could copy the amenities. Four Seasons was, in fact, the first chain to put shampoo in the showers and the first to ensure that every room had a functional desk and two-line telephone. Those ideas were soon copied. Today even the cheapest and most basic budget hotel offers shampoo in the bathroom. He needed a strategy to truly differentiate the Four Seasons experience. The breakthrough idea was that luxury was a combination of design and amenities with truly personalized, courteous, friendly service. Great service is relatively easy to achieve in a singular hotel and, on the good days, in many properties. It is really difficult to achieve across the globe all day every day, week after week and year after year. The only way to achieve that difficult standard was to engage each staff member at every property. And, in his view, the only way to do that is to treat each staff member in a way that makes them want to engage. The famous Four Seasons values are built around the golden rule: to seek to deal with others as we would have them deal with us.

The linkages across these three components are so tight that they can be thought of in any direction. In my explanation I went from *vision* to the strategy embedded in the *plan* to the *values* needed to achieve it. But one could start anywhere and move in any direction. One could start in the hotel business with a strong set of values about how people should be treated. That could lead to the idea that a truly engaged workforce – 24/7, around the world – would be a strategic differentiator that could lead to the audacious thought that it was possible to build the world's leading luxury hotel chain on personalized service. No one will ever know for sure how the Four Seasons pattern was created – from the strategic insight, from the audacious vision, from a conviction about how people should be treated. When the linkage is tight, the order does not matter. Everything just fits.

Another very impressive businessperson who appeared at the school was A.G. Lafley of P&G. A.G. took over P&G when it was beginning to struggle. He did a remarkable job of putting that company back on its path and in its place as one of the world's greatest-ever consumer goods companies. In *The Game-Changer*, the book he wrote with Ram Charan, he said that his company (and possibly by extension all great companies) is "purpose-led and values-driven." His purpose for P&G was to be a company that "improves the lives of ordinary people in small but meaningful ways." That vision was accompanied by a set of espoused values built on obsession with the consumer, with finding small or large ways to make the life of an ordinary person just a little better. The vision and value were then translated into concrete business activity by the idea that P&G would be driven by innovation – defined as the development and marketing of products that were used repeatedly. Innovation was a great differentiating strategy idea. P&G had exceptional technical skills as well an unparalleled global sales and marketing infrastructure. It was also the expression of the idea that consumers' lives should be made better, not just maintained at the current level made possible by earlier innovations. And it was a call for all P&Gers to get truly engaged and take a real service mindset with consumers, to imagine the ways that their lives could be improved. Again, it is possible to put those ideas together in any order. It could be a strategic idea, then true differentiating competitive advantage, made inspiring by a soaring vision statement, making people's lives better, and a call to engagement with supporting values of integrity and respect. Or one could start with engaging values and go back to the vision those values would support, and then consider what strategy would make it all a business success that could deliver on the promise year after year. When the connection is tight, the order doesn't matter. The power is in the consistency.

The leadership lesson from these examples follows. If you want to lead, you have to have an idea – a vision – and you have to have people accept those ideas because they are attached to a set of values that people can believe in, and then you have to have a winning strategy or it will all be for naught. Another way to arrive at the same place is to envisage that you have come up with a great strategy for achieving some objective – better software, a better sustaining customer mix, a higher score on some internal metric. If you need a group of people to be with you in executing that strategy, you have to connect it to a meaningful purpose, a vision of where it will all lead. And that vision will have both meaning and attraction if it is associated with a set of values which makes people feel that the sacrifices they might make to achieve the vision are worthwhile.

The examples also illustrate an important principle. Leadership is pragmatic and practical. Leaders may have great dreams, but they need a winning strategy or it remains a dream. Leaders may have a great strategic idea for the delivery of a particular business or service, but it has to be connected to a bigger and more compelling vision if people are to be induced to become enthusiastic proponents. And it has to tap into some set of values to produce real engagement.

The next set of linkages to explore is what I think of as the middle set. The plan, vision, and values make it clear where we are going and why; the next step is to get people to work to make it all happen. Getting people to work means that they are assembled and organized, understand the task, and are ready to go. There are many aspects of the Four Seasons approach that illustrate this point, but they do it in a different way than many other global service-based businesses. Many service organizations strive for quality by making everything consistent. This enables training programs to be very specific and the product offering to be uniform and predictable. McDonald's and the entire fast-food industry are great exemplars of this approach. It enables the delivery of the "brand promise" in many locations, with large numbers of very

Figure 7.2. Organize – Alignment – Clarity: horizontal linkages

MANAGING	DIRECTING	ENGAGING
ORGANIZE	ALIGNMENT	CLARITY

different and very diverse staff groups. Four Seasons is different. Each property is unique. They manage less than 100 properties, not the tens of thousands of a fast-food chain. They do have service standards, but they are about behavior and attitude, such as smile, make eye contact, and use the guest's name as much as they are about how many times the phone rings before it is picked up. They do have auditable operating standards, but they want their staff to meet those standards with their own style and personality. And that has turned out to be a great way to organize when the foundation of the strategy is to have each member of the staff feel empowered and responsible for the service experience of each guest. That can't happen if service is routinized. And it can't happen unless everyone "buys into" – which is to say, is aligned with – the vision and values.

Each property is managed by a general manager whose compensation includes a significant bonus, based as much on employee attitudes and service quality as on profitability. To ensure each employee around the world treated the right way, each and every manager has to believe in the Four Seasons values. In many parts of the world, this means that the managers must rise above their own cultural norms and backgrounds, which may favor status and privilege or prescribed gender roles, in favor of the corporate values of treating everyone with the same courtesy and respect. A general manager in the Four Seasons system has to make a significant commitment to communication. Regular meetings with all staff reinforce the Four Seasons vision and values. And Four Seasons is very clear about how it wants things done. There is absolute clarity

about the operating standards. When they took over the Hotel George
V hotel in Paris and closed it for a two-year renovation, many won-
dered how they would deal with the notoriously prickly, unionized
workforce. From day one they treated their new employees the same as
all other Four Seasons employees, giving them the right to come back
to the hotel when the renovations were finished. And then they trained,
trained, and trained them to perform the Four Seasons way.

P&G is famous for its product innovations, its brands, and its marketing prowess. Few are as aware that it has also been, throughout its
history, one of the most innovative companies in the area of organization design. P&G invented the brand manager idea, was the first to develop a global matrix of product category and country, and continues to
be a company dedicated to promoting from within. When A.G. Lafley
took the top job, P&G was in the midst of another organization design
revolution, combining a classic country-based organization structure
with a global product system and global business service groups. The
design was bold and unproven, but it fit with the focus on innovation
and reinforced the alignment that was being sought with that vision
and strategy. And A.G. was clear about how innovation would be measured at P&G. Innovation was not about coming up with new products.
Innovation was about new products that became repeat purchases by
consumers. This gave clarity to the two parts of the organization. The
Global Business Units developed products that would delight consumers so that they would become repeat purchasers. The country-based
Market Development Group would ensure that the products were
properly promoted and merchandised on the shelf.

The new organization structure clarified the vision. It meant developing new products that tangibly and recognizably make people's lives
better *and* getting them on the right shelf in the right outlets at the right
price. Both have to happen for the vision to be realized. A.G. called this
the "two moments of truth." The structure gave clarity to that idea. And
defining innovation as repeat purchases made by a pleased customer
gave the entire organization clarity about what was to be expected. This
description of the P&G system goes from left to right along the middle
row of the model. Organize this way to align duties with the vision,

Figure 7.3. Control – Motivation – Involvement: horizontal linkages

MANAGING	DIRECTING	ENGAGING
CONTROL	MOTIVATION	INVOLVEMENT

bringing clarity to the expected outcome. But one could have described it in the other direction. A.G. might have started with a clear idea of what a successful innovation would look like. He would then work to ensure that the organization was aligned with that idea, reinforced with an organization design that focused on each step of the process. The model works when the relationship between each component is so tight that it can operate in any direction. Each component reinforces the other and each is a way to translate the plan, vision, and values into action.

The final set of horizontal linkages is the Control – Motivation – Involvement set. In some senses this is a set of activities that a leader can look at somewhat passively as the ultimate leader's report card. Control gets at the question about whether desired results are being achieved. Did you come up with a winning strategy? Motivation gets at whether people are performing with purpose and intent to do things the right way. Are people aligned with the vision? Involvement is the observation of whether people are working with energy, taking initiatives and appropriate risks, without being asked, taking ownership for the success of the entire enterprise. Do people believe in the values of the organization and have clarity about how they can contribute?

Looking at this set passively as simply a report card is useful, but it undermines the value of being active along each of these dimensions. If we come back to Four Seasons, an exemplar of a well-led enterprise, there is evidence of considerable thought and attention to each of them. Four Seasons uses both internal and external auditors to check on how each property is performing. The audit teams visit each property with the 270 core standards and Four Seasons service culture standards clearly in hand. Because Four Seasons people tend to stay with the company for a long time, most would not have to look in the manual to know each and every one. They live the standards. If there is any doubt about what a standard means or how it should be applied, the audit will provide the clarification. Control is an active process that makes things happen. In addition, every hotel general manager has a meeting each day with the senior staff to go over what they call "the glitch report" about some moment the previous day when a guest's service expectations were not met. At the end of every week a summary of the week's glitches and the process improvements to ensure that they do not happen again is sent to head office. A nil report or a report that there were no glitches that week is not considered a good thing because it meant something was being overlooked.

Motivation is assessed in many ways. Part of every general manager's bonus is attached to the results of the regular employee survey. Stories of employees who go "above and beyond" are circulated and lauded. Staff, including their families, is invited to the hotel to experience its special qualities. Celebrations of milestones or great results achieved are part of the way that business is done. But Four Seasons also recognizes that it takes organization to get people fully involved every day in the business. Perhaps a story will illustrate the point.

A colleague was working with an organization in Vancouver. He was there for three days and was fortunate enough that this client put him up at the Four Seasons. He spent the morning with the client and the afternoon in his room doing his follow-up and preparatory work for the next day. His room was comfortable and well appointed. Room service was excellent. Why go anywhere else? The room had a lovely view of what may be the world's most beautiful city with the mountains coming down to the ocean. He set his chair up near the window with the light coming in over his shoulder. Heaven!

Many months later he returned to Vancouver and was again able to stay at the Four Seasons. He checked into his room and, much to his surprise, found that the furniture was arranged the way that he left it on his earlier visit. How did that happen? The furniture had not been left carelessly out of place for many months. It was, of course, not even the same room. Someone had done something.

As you think through that story, try to imagine the chain of events that created it. The person making up his room had observed that the furniture was moved. When it was done for the second time, the housekeeper noted that it was something this guest liked. She (probably a she) recognized that there might be an opportunity here to do something very special for this guest, and she did not want to let it go by. Now there had to be a procedure enabling her to collect that information and pass it along to someone else. If there was no procedure it would have been noted but lost. The procedure then had to have the picture of the furniture arrangement entered into a system so that if this guest ever returned it would be noted. When he did return, someone had to notice the special entry, reserve a particular room, and send instructions to the person preparing that room about how to arrange the furniture. At that point the housekeeper would have added to the heavy job of lifting mattresses and cleaning bathrooms the task of ensuring the furniture was moved to the right place. The result: an absolutely delighted guest.

It is worth noting that all that work was done behind the scenes by people who would never know the guest's reaction and never directly profit from doing it. The first housekeeper never saw the guest and would certainly not think that by entering information in a system her tip would increase. The person entering the information in the system would have no expectation that my colleague would ever return. The person making up the room would have no assurance that the guest would particularly notice or care. So many little steps were taken by people who were not doing it for immediate or tangible reward but for the more powerful idea that "this is what makes my work special and this is what makes me special."

This is a story that sticks with me when I work with organizations in many different fields. I ask people in health care, how can it be so hard to get basic life-enhancing information passed from one unit to the next? I ask people in education how often a school gets everyone involved in the four- or eight-year journey that each student takes passing through that critical stage of life. I ask people in industry how often they are able to pass a customer from one department to another without tying it to some kind of bonus scheme that is eventually gamed. Inevitably I look around the room and see heads hanging down. The Four Seasons story is meant to illustrate a number of points. It takes values to get an engaged workforce. But it can't stop there. It takes hard concrete work. Systems and procedures have to be in place. Leave out just one and it does not happen. It might be as simple as a scrap of paper to chart out how the furniture was arranged. It might be a software package that enables this "soft" information to be easily stored and retrieved. It is certainly a guest-centered information system that recognizes my colleague as a unique individual, with unique but not earth-shaking needs. And it gets reinforced when the person making up his room gets the notice about how the furniture is to be arranged. That is the quiet symbol that someone is watching and listening, and when guest preferences are noted, something happens.

Involvement does not just happen. It is energized by the vision and values. It is focused by the clarity about where involvement is needed and appropriate. It is driven by people who are aligned and motivated. But it has to be facilitated and organized. In fact, while in the previous sections I have pointed out how the connections across the elements are so tight that one can start with any of them and connect it to the others, in this case, the connections are even tighter.

One way of thinking about leadership is as an exercise in inducing energized, focused involvement from anyone and everyone who can play a part in making some desired action happen. The person who is really involved knows and believes in the vision and wants to do what is required to make it happen. The person who is productively involved knows the plan, knows what role they play in its execution, and can see the hard results that are measured so they know how success is assessed. The involved person has clarity about what is to be done and about the latitude they might have in determining how to do it. And the involved person knows intellectually and feels emotionally what the values are to guide independent action. As an example, Four Seasons has a standard about leaving a hot coffeepot on the table so that each guest can keep their own cup full when they want to. But Four

Figure 7.4. Universal linkages: alignment as the focus and the goal

MANAGING	DIRECTING	ENGAGING
PLAN	VISION	VALUES
ORGANIZE	ALIGNMENT	CLARITY
CONTROL	MOTIVATION	INVOLVEMENT

Seasons in Paris, operated as Hotel George V, knows that in France that it considered poor service. They bend the hotel standard but then have to use another process to pay particular attention to ensure the guest's cup is never empty.

Project Leadership

I have built this chapter around Four Seasons because it such a great example of a well-led company. But of course the model would not be very interesting or useful if it was just about building a well-led company. In my view it works everywhere. Consider, for example, a person who had been tasked with leading a team, perhaps to improve a process, perhaps to bring a new service to market, perhaps to improve overall customer experience. The team is assembled from across the enterprise. Each individual comes with different perspectives, skills, and expertise. Some will be highly motivated to be on the team. Some will consider it just another assignment. Some will wish they could go back to their day job. The team leader has to find a way to get everyone involved or the project is not likely to be successful, and the failure of a team project usually sits on the shoulders of the named leader.

Most project teams have little trouble with the managing side of the framework. An overall plan is sketched out with timelines and resource requirements. Checkpoints are established to keep control of the activities and ensure that everyone is informed about what is happening. But many on the team will be conflicted. Their own departments and their own lives may be affected by the outcome of the project. Whatever the outcome, it is all extra work for which they may not receive any credit or recognition from the people in charge of their careers or compensation. They may be unmotivated.

I am always impressed by how quickly and easily people from all backgrounds and experiences get at the managing tasks. People in health care who have been brought up with a science background do it naturally. People in education or child services have a project administration mindset that fits easily into management roles. But I am equally surprised at how few groups naturally recognize the critical role of leadership in making a project team function. Teams do not lead themselves. The splintering forces are very powerful. The effective team leader will work hard to ensure that there is a clear and compelling vision for the project and will spend the time to ensure that each member of the team is aligned, which is to say that each team member understands and agree with the vision. Some people call this the team charter. It spells out explicitly the shared sense of purpose and interdependency. It keeps people motivated by the higher purpose of the project. In effective teams someone does this work. Often it is the person designated as team leader, but the "real" leader of the team may be a team member who simply recognizes that teams need the fundamentals of leadership and steps up to fill the perceived gap.

Effective, pragmatic team leaders will also recognize that the tools of engagement can be the most effective motivators available to them. One of the reasons people do their best work in project teams is that those assignments give them the opportunity to engage, whereas most of their regular job is about following procedures and directives from above. From the beginning the effective team leader will be clear about the values on which the team will build. The values could be about collaboration. They could be about respecting the skills and capabilities of the team members. They could be about breaking down silos to put the company (or the customer, or the employees) first. They could be about providing an opportunity for each team member to acquire a new skill or network or reputation. There are lots of values to work with. The effective, pragmatic leader will think hard about the ones that will be most useful in achieving the desired result and then be assiduous in ensuring that they are always respected, observed, and celebrated. The effective team leader will also ensure that there is clarity about what the project will and will not cover. Project scope has a way of creeping, resulting in the original mandate not being met. People on the team need to know where they can and should focus their effort and initiative.

Being a project team leader is often a make-or-break opportunity for the upwardly ambitious middle manager. It is the opportunity to demonstrate capability to senior management. It is the opportunity to get outside a functional or geographic box and see the enterprise as a whole. It is an opportunity to build a new network. A lot can be riding on the assignment. As I said at the beginning, the leader's job is to get results. In the end, the project team leader will be judged by the perceived strength of the team's work and the actions that follow. The effective and pragmatic team leader will know that the way to get the best result is to create a team that is engaged, knows where it is going, and does its work – engaged, directed, and managed.

The Leadership Grid at Work .

One group of former students returned to the classroom to talk about how they use the leadership model. The group came from the senior leadership team of a public education district. They told the class that when they use the model they always start at the top right, in the Vision

Figure 7.5. Vision – Values – Clarity

MANAGING	DIRECTING	ENGAGING
PLAN	VISION	VALUES
ORGANIZE	ALIGNMENT	CLARITY
CONTROL	MOTIVATION	INVOLVEMENT

– Values – Clarity cluster. In their view it is essential to get that cluster right before proceeding any further. They use the model as a guide to the implementation of any new initiative at the school district.

Clarity at the Top

They start by ensuring that they all know how to articulate the purpose of the new initiative in words that everyone involved can relate to and understand. Then they think through the values that this initiative is favoring. Everything in public education touches on some set of values that is being preferred over another. Initiatives to increase average test scores speak to a value of ensuring students are prepared for the world but can be unproductive for other values, like building self-esteem and keeping students in school longer. It is important to get these possible values clarified. Then they think through the "must dos" and distinguish them from the elements of the new directive that can be left to the discretion and

Figure 7.6. Plan – Alignment – Involvement

MANAGING	DIRECTING	ENGAGING
PLAN	VISION	VALUES
ORGANIZE	ALIGNMENT	CLARITY
CONTROL	MOTIVATION	INVOLVEMENT

initiative of the teacher in the classroom. No teacher is going to teach from a prepared script, but there must be clarity on what they must do. They go back and forth in these three boxes until they have words that fit.

Get Ready to Go

With those three boxes in hand, they can proceed to working out an implementation plan, paying attention to who has to be aligned and how that alignment will be achieved. That work enables them to be clear about where and how individual involvement can be facilitated and allowed.

Get to Work

At that point they think through what organizational arrangements may be required, from hiring and job descriptions to processes and

Figure 7.7. Organize – Motivation

MANAGING	DIRECTING	ENGAGING
PLAN	VISION	VALUES
ORGANIZE	ALIGNMENT	CLARITY
CONTROL	MOTIVATION	INVOLVEMENT

procedures, and how they will motivate people to actually do what has to be done.

Keep It on Track

All of that work ends up in the Control box, which comes last, not because it is least important but because one does not know what to control until it is clear what has to be done.

This story from a team of my former students resonates with the amazing story of Google, a company that has, over the past decade, become such a global phenomenon that "google" is a recognized verb. What started as a better search engine is a now a powerhouse of applications from email, maps, and street views to file storage to driverless cars and Google "glasses." It is an amazing story. And from all the stories that I read, including *How Google Works*, the bestselling book by Eric Schmidt and Jonathan Rosenberg (two of its former most senior

Figure 7.8. Control

MANAGING	DIRECTING	ENGAGING
PLAN	VISION	VALUES
ORGANIZE	ALIGNMENT	CLARITY
CONTROL	MOTIVATION	INVOLVEMENT

operating executives who are now advisors to the firm), Google is a company that works because, from the beginning, there was clarity in the vision of "organizing the world's information" and in the values – from "focus on the user and all else will follow" to the value stated as "you can make money without doing evil." From that foundation they have rigorous plans for everything that they do, work hard at having people aligned and involved, are well organized and motivated, and keep track of everything using their own systems and technology.

Whether we look at a large enterprise (a company, hospital, school district, or public service organization), a unit within it (division, department, school, or office), or a group assembled for a particular task, we can see opportunities for leadership. Enterprises, units, and groups that are successful in the sense of delivering results at or above expectation inevitably are well led. The person or people doing the leading may be very different. They may be outgoing or introverted. They may exude confidence or anxiety. They may be great communicators or careful listeners. They may have large dreams or be tightly focused. Leaders come in all shapes and sizes. The well-led part of leadership is not about these surface attributes. It is about what they do with the skills and attributes that they have. The model that I have built focuses on what effective leaders do. They manage so that everyone knows the plan and their own role in achieving it. They provide direction and use the tools necessary to align people to and motivate them in the pursuit of that direction. They find a way to engage everyone to bring their best to the job every day by associating the work with worthwhile values, providing clarity on the work to be done, and ensuring that the mechanisms are in place to allow people to be involved.

Leadership is tough work for those who choose to try to do it well. There will be many days when it is hard to see how everything will come together. And there will be discouraging days when it does not come together. The model I have built pulls together the various elements that have to be considered and acted on in consistent and coordinated ways to increase the chances that the outcome will be a positive one. It is not easy but it is not impossible. It does require deep, hard thought.

Chapter Eight

LEADERSHIP 360

Saving a Parrot

Paul Butler is a remarkable individual. In 1977, he spent a summer completing a field research expedition in St. Lucia. During that expedition he studied the St. Lucia parrot, a gorgeous bird found only on that island and facing extinction from the usual pressures of habitat destruction, hunters, and pet trappers. Before he left the island he wrote a report with recommendations for preserving the species. On graduation, he was offered a six-month job as a conservation advisor to the St. Lucia forestry department to see if he could implement his recommendations and save the bird. His recommendations were just what one would expect: enact tougher conservation laws; provide enough trained and equipped staff to enforce them; extend legally mandated forest sanctuaries. These are all good ideas and the foundation of species protection efforts around the world. The problem is that he needed the government to enact the laws and provide the resources. To get that support he needed to get the St. Lucian people to demand action. He needed the various stakeholders in tourism, agriculture, and logging to support the idea or at least not oppose it. He needed other environmental agencies and NGOs to support his cause as well as their own. He needed widespread, voluntary compliance. He needed people to report infractions, stop turning their heads, and pressure companies and their own representatives to do the right thing. In short, he needed to lead in all directions.

The story of Paul Butler has parallels in the story of leadership in all situations: Leadership 360. We often picture leadership as a vertical set of interactions, responding to direction from above and motivating the troops below. In fact, leadership is virtually always a 360-degree activity, responding to the web of interdependencies that characterizes life today. People who are called, or think of themselves as, leaders usually do have a group for whom they have primary responsibility. But they also have to "lead" their boss or bosses in the sense of influencing or persuading that person or those persons that what they are doing is right under the circumstances and is worthy of support, appropriate resources, and a realistic timeline. They will also have many support groups (perhaps customers, perhaps suppliers), all of whom have to come together if anything is going to happen. And Paul Butler's is just such a story.

He set out to make an emotional case with the people of St. Lucia that they were the kind of people who protected their own assets. Using a variety of tactics he was able to convince St. Lucians that protecting the St. Lucia parrot was something they wanted to do. With public support, laws were passed. Local industry came on his side and voluntarily complied. People became the police, watching for and reporting infractions. Enforcement agencies pursued offenders because the community demanded it. The parrot was saved because Paul Butler led the entire nation to rally around this cause.

Paul Butler stayed for 10 years with the forestry department of St. Lucia, leaving to join RarePlanet, an organization devoted to energizing communities for environmental and conservation causes. In 1988 the same methodology was used to save the St. Vincent parrot. By 2000, with 30 programs behind it, the methodology, now labeled PRIDE, was embedded in university curricula. By 2007 over 100 such programs had been launched around the world. RarePlanet, now called simply Rare, continues to inspire communities to take care of the environment and each other by leading all the stakeholders and interested parties to come together around a common cause.

Restoring Mental Health Services

The leadership idea embedded in PRIDE is that in order to make anything significant happen it is necessary to identify all the parties that can help or hinder and to find ways to align them with the cause. Are these ideas useful in the workplace? Consider this story from a former student. The names and place has been changed to protect anonymity but the rest is as it happened.

In May 1995, Greg Robertson was faced with the biggest leadership challenge of his young professional life. Greg was a speech language pathologist at Great Lakes Regional Health Centre. In 1993 he had moved on from direct patient service through various administrative positions to become manager of a unit of 80 professionals delivering different kinds of rehabilitation and mental health services. It was a varied group with lots of competing interests. Greg got the job because, in his words, speech language therapists were considered the least powerful and therefore the least objectionable professionals for the position.

In May 1995, an entire team of five adult-care psychiatrists – the backbone of the mental health team – announced that they would all be resigning at the end of June, leaving a 34-bed unit unstaffed. The psychiatrists had a legitimate beef. The unit was understaffed. The hospital was in an area with a rapidly growing population. The emergency room was extremely busy, with one doctor handling, on average, 10 new patients an hour. Stressed and overworked, the emergency room physicians coped by routinely referring any patient with mental health symptoms to the psychiatrist on call. This meant that every fifth night, all year long, psychiatrists would be up all night in the emergency room before conducting their normal practice the next day. Once the patient was referred and accepted, the unit only had enough staff for pharmaceutical treatment and custodial care before discharge. There was no facility for alternative treatments or outpatient care. It was a stressful, unhappy unit. When one psychiatrist left to go into personal practice, he demonstrated that a more satisfying personal and professional life was possible. His example made the current situation even more untenable for the psychiatrists on staff. It was impossible to recruit new professional staff into this environment and, with so much tension in the unit, it had been impossible to persuade the government funding agency to provide the resources necessary to create meaningful change.

As soon as Greg heard the news of the impending resignations, he went into action. Under the motto "Failure is not an option," taken from the Apollo 13 story, he set about to lead toward a new service model which met the needs of the community, respected the role of Great Lakes as a full-service regional hospital, and created a satisfying professional working environment. The first step was to create and lead a working group to deal with current issues and plan for the future. As that group went to work though, it was imperative to get the support of senior management, the board, the government funding agency, the surrounding hospitals, and community service organizations. Since everything flowed through the emergency room, that group had to be committed to a final solution. Local general practitioners had to be part of the solution. Finally, although they had all resigned, the psychiatrists were a continuing concern. Greg needed some or all of them to return to make the new service work, and he needed to ensure that they did not become a force that discouraged new professional staff from joining. It was a daunting list of stakeholders to lead, but leaving out any one of them would almost guarantee the failure of any proposed solution. And although each of the stakeholders had a different interest and a different perspective, each had to agree with and support the final solution.

Greg and the group had to create a vision of mental health service that would work from all points of view. They needed all parties aligned with their vision and motivated to help in its achievement. In the health world there are many skeptics. There are more than enough lofty visions in health care and too few practical working solutions. The board and management had to be convinced that it was not better to let another hospital take care of the mental health programs. The government agency that funds the hospital had to be convinced that there was a financially viable solution. Support staff had to be convinced that this was not an excuse for another round of layoffs. The non-psychiatric medical staff had to be convinced that it was worth helping the mental health unit get back on its feet. Psychiatrists had to be convinced that

Great Lakes would provide a personally and professionally satisfactory place to practice. Other hospitals in the community, who had picked up the pieces after everything fell apart, had to agree to leave room for Great Lakes in the spectrum of mental health service delivery.

Greg and his team worked through each element of the integrated framework to find a solution that met all these needs for all the parties. It was a classic Leadership 360 event. Unless everyone was on the same side, no solution would work. They communicated endlessly – for several months there was a daily telephone update available to all who dialed in. They built heavily on the values of meeting the needs of the community and of providing full patient-centered care.

In September, less than three months after the mass resignations, 10 beds were reopened. Two psychiatrists returned. Family physicians were organized to provide the on-call support. Various agencies were aligned to provide follow-up care in the community. Five years later there was a thriving service with 23 beds and numerous new services provided in the community – Leadership 360 in action!

The Reality of Leadership

The classic picture of the leader is of the person with responsibility for a group organized to achieve a mission. The task of the leader is to get that group – always made up of diverse people with unique hopes and aspirations, personal lives outside work, and different backgrounds and values – to come together around a common vision and the shared values that will get the work done. This is a powerful force when it is done well. This entire book develops and explains a model that integrates the various elements making up the work of leadership. The model contains the very specific things that a thoughtful leader can do to bring the group together and increase the probability that the task will be accomplished. It is hard work, but it is not impossible for anyone with the will and the courage to try.

But the reality of leadership is even more complicated and difficult than that. Picture yourself as a middle manager in any kind of enterprise. You have a team of 15 or 20 people who refer to you as boss. You are one of a group of six or eight who report to someone else whom you call boss. But you also work within an organization that has a purchasing department, human resources, legal, and information technology, to mention just a few of the many people on whom your team relies to get the job done. Then there is the senior management group, the ones that you hardly know, the ones that you present your plans and projects to once or twice a year, the ones whose support you really need to get the corporate resources, realistic deadlines, and mandates to make things happen. But wait, there are more – there are the customers you serve, inside and outside the organization. There are key suppliers who can get your team what it needs when it really needs it – or not. There is the community within which you work – the neighbors, the municipality, and the governments at different levels, with their service workers, inspectors, regulators, and helpers. If you want to achieve anything that really matters, the entire group has to either get on your side or get out of the way.

That does sound like a complicated job. Middle management is complicated. How much easier must it be to finally get to the top of the ladder, to be the CEO, the managing director? At that level all those staff groups with all their rules and procedures work for you. It is tempting to contemplate this picture with a certain degree of longing, to pine for the moment when you are the boss of all the bosses, when there are fewer people to get on your side and more people to boss, when you hold more of the motivational keys in your own hands. And yet what I have heard, over and over, from the most senior of executives, is their longing to return to the middle-management jobs of their early career, when they felt that they really had the opportunity to "get things done." It is the most senior of executives, the ones with apparently the most power, who feel the most powerless. They are the ones who feel caught in a web of dependencies – on the whims of the capital markets, on a central funder, on government regulation, action, or inaction, on the loyalty of key employees, on the integrity and commitment of customers and suppliers, and on the simple capability of key people in critical positions. For the truth is that everyone has a boss. Everyone is part of a web of dependencies. The more that success is determined by creativity, energy, and initiative, the more powerless the boss becomes and the more dependent on leadership skills.

So if leadership happens at the top and the middle, does it happen everywhere? Are there stress-free places at the front line, with the person who is actually doing the work – the customer service representative (CSR) in a bank, the bedside nurse, the teacher in a classroom? Surely there are jobs where one can just perform and not lead. And aren't there technical jobs where one can simply do the work and go home? But wait: the front-line worker is also part of a web of interdependencies. The technician is doing the work for someone and always has to rely on the work of someone else. The CSR has transactions to perform but also has a customer in front of them with needs and questions, which require answers from another part of the bank. And the nurse has a really complicated job. The nurse has to induce a number of allied and independent professionals to coordinate their work to serve the patient. The nurse has to lead the family through the medical journey and has to coordinate with the nurses who cover other shifts to ensure a consistent approach. The teacher may be able to close the door and just work with the class but will also be looking for resources from others and may be dealing with parents, trying to lead them to a more productive relationship with their child. The technicians get their assignment from a person, and their solutions only work if they permit other humans to perform something effectively.

The fact is that in the working world we are all part of a web of human interdependencies: receiving demands, requirements, resources, and limitations from one set of people and passing similar requests and interventions on to others. Perhaps the difference is that at some levels there is more opportunity for choosing to lead; at others it is an unavoidable obligation. Typically, at the front line, the less effective worker can simply accept the rules and given resources and go no further, passing conflicts and issues up the line for others to deal with. The nurse can simply do a good job at the bedside, follow the written orders, and go home or on to the next part-time assignment, leaving the coordination of care to others. The CSR can do the transactions and follow the rule book for everything else, and when in doubt, send the customer to the next person up the line. The teacher can simply follow the curriculum and all the associated guidelines and send the child with other issues to the vice principal. The technician can avoid human interaction, simply accept the assignment and its constraints, do the best possible job, and move on.

The point of all this is that there are opportunities to lead at all levels of any enterprise. On the front line one can choose to let the opportunities go by, albeit it at a cost to the overall success of the enterprise. At the higher levels, there is no place to hide. There, done well or done poorly, leading is the job. The ideal is an organization that treats everyone as leader, where everyone accepts the role within their own sphere of influence. If leadership of the enterprise is successful, as we go down the ladder, each person, each leader, will create his or her own leadership plan in a way that nests it within the leadership plan of the person above.

Lead the Operating Team, Customers, Suppliers, and the Community

The Leadership 360 idea – leading from the middle – is shown in Figure 8.1. As shown in the figure, the leader in the middle needs different things from different parties, and each party has different expectations of the leader. It is important to note, though, that the web of needs and dependencies form a pattern where the same things that serve one party also serve another. Look at the chart from the perspective of the middle manager – the engine room of most organizations. The middle manager – nurse manager, clinic manager, principal, office manager, team lead, or section head – leads the operating team, a group of people who are the front face working with customers, clients, users, suppliers, and the community. The leader needs that group to conduct the business, deal with problems, and build productive relationships. But the leader also has to think through how to lead customers, suppliers, and the community in which the enterprise operates. It may seem unusual to think about leadership in the context of customers, but the essence of the brand promise, the reason for buying, is the expectation of a certain customer experience. The customer needs to know what that

Figure 8.1. Leading in all directions

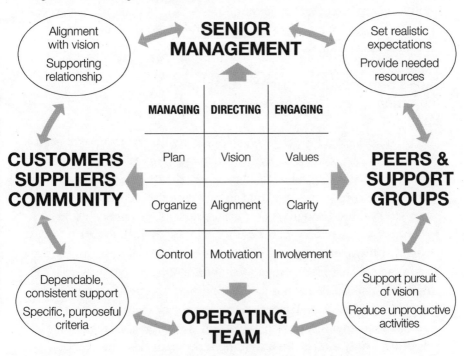

expectation is, in the same way that the team needs to be clear what it is expected to deliver. It is also unusual to think about leadership in the context of supplier relationships. But again, if an enterprise is going to have a productive relationship with its suppliers, they too need to know how the enterprise expects to be served and what values are expressed in the relationship. Well-led units work with a consistency that sends that powerful, though often unstated, message. The same consistency of purpose and values underpins the relationship between an enterprise and its communities. When a community grows to know what to expect from an enterprise and from any interaction, it is possible to build a productive relationship. When the community sees one approach one day and another the next, when the mantra in the community is "it depends on who you talk to," then suspicion builds, small incidents become large ones, and everyone is on their guard. Consistency comes from a well-led enterprise because everyone knows where the unit is going, is engaged in getting it there, and is working in an organized way on a plan. The power of well-led organizations like Four Seasons and P&G is this clarity and consistency.

Lead Senior Management, Customers, Suppliers, and the Community

As we move around the chart we can also see the congruence of needs of senior management with those of customers, suppliers, and the community. Senior management needs to know that the unit is operating to achieve the corporate vision and in a way that is consistent with the corporate values. Though senior management has an oversight and control function to perform, in the daily operation of the business it has to trust that the operating units and support services are performing appropriately (of course, it also has to hope that they are performing at the highest possible level – not just getting by). The primary tool senior management has at its disposal to increase the chance that expectations are met is its own leadership skills. If the enterprise is aligned to the vision and fully engaged in pursuing it the right way, the chances improve that the performance will be satisfactory, or even more than satisfactory. Effective leadership from senior management comes from giving clear direction, supporting activities that are aligned with the vision, and rewarding the right kinds of behaviors. Customers, suppliers, and the community respond to the same kind of stimuli as senior management. Each of these parties is looking for consistent behavior that is appropriate to the situation and, in return, is more likely to respond with consistent behavior.

Lead Senior Management, Peers, and Support Groups

Continuing on then, consider the congruence of senior management and the peer and support relationships that exist within an organization. The operating unit needs resources and assistance from senior management to achieve its goals. It also needs both senior management and the support units to have realistic expectations of what the unit can achieve. If senior management sets targets that are beyond reach, it risks either disengagement of the unit or the silent encouragement of inappropriate behavior. But senior management takes its cue about what can be delivered from the explicit leadership skills of the team leader. Leading up is a requirement of middle managers. Support units can also create similar problems and opportunities. If support units set rules and expectations that are inconsistent with the rhythm of the businesses, they are tacitly encouraging either disengagement from the work to be done or an atmosphere of ignoring or working around rules of procedure. Neither is conducive to an engaged organization. As an example, frequently there are rules and procedures for major procurement that are inconsistent with the reality of the business, especially in publicly funded enterprises. There may be a demand for multiple bids when there are only one or two credible suppliers. Or there may be a requirement for a formal "request for proposal" purchasing process when it is not possible to set out realistic and complete expectations for the supplier to bid on. In those circumstances two things are likely to happen: If people are really committed to the purpose, a great deal of unproductive energy will be spent figuring out how to get around the rules to get the job done. Some call this "doing the right thing." On the other hand, if people are just going through the motions (doing things right), the rules will be followed but performance will suffer. It is interesting to note as an example that years after the devastating earthquakes in Haiti, there is still a great deal of fundamental clean-up and rebuilding to be done. The explanation seems to be that the procurement systems for hiring people to organize and perform the clean-up takes a long time to develop and is taking a long time to implement. The only action that has taken place is from the few NGOs with their own resources who simply get things done.

Lead the Operating Team, Peers, and Support Groups

Finally, we can look at the similarity between what the team itself expects and needs and what peer and support organizations expect and need. Teams and support organizations need to know where the unit is headed and how it intends to get there if they are expected to provide engaged direct activity or engaged support. There really is not that much difference between the work of a person in a unit and the work of a person in a support organization assigned to that unit, with one important exception. The support unit person will have competing priorities and will often be expected to provide some kind of quality oversight of the way support resources are being used. In either case, the effective leader knows that the people have the same needs and the same demands on their leader. They need to be aligned and motivated to achieve the unit's vision. They need to know the plan and where they fit in, and they need to be engaged with all the same tools of Values – Clarity – Involvement.

Leadership 360: Be Consistent

There are two implication of this analysis of the leadership task. The first: the leader has to recognize that each of these groups has to be led. Thinking about the job as being primarily or exclusively about building and leading the operating team itself is just not sufficient. The second: the overlap in needs of each group requires one consistent approach – a holistic approach. There has to be consistency of message in all directions. It does not work to have senior management believe that the unit is following one path while the people in the unit are really following another. This is usually the root of the maverick division approach, where a particular leader believes that top management is wrong and he or she is right. The leader tells top management what it wants to hear while telling the team what the leader believes is the right way to go. The sincere desire of the maverick leader to act this way could have its roots in a number of honorable places, but it inevitably comes to grief. Overzealous and unrealistic support groups can induce maverick behavior from the most committed. Weak or inconsistent senior leadership can produce the same result. The maverick leader is usually very well intentioned. The problems arise with the overlaps. The support groups hear one thing when they work with the people in the unit and another when they work with senior management. Customers and suppliers hear one thing when they work with the unit and another when they work at the corporate level or with senior management. The only way to get all the needed constituents working to make the unit as productive as possible is to lead consistently in all directions.

For the working leader this takes us all the way back to the beginning, to seeing leadership as hard, thoughtful work. For the thoughtful leader there is no consistency problem. Telling one story in one direction and another story where it seems to suit them is simply not the way that thoughtful people work. The thoughtful leader will take the time to get clarity of purpose and direction from senior management and will confront the issues of inconsistent and unrealistic approaches from the support groups rather than working around or against them. The thoughtful leader will also call on all available emotional intelligence tools to determine how best to approach and work consistently with the different groups. It is unlikely that support groups are deliberately setting out to make it impossible for an operating unit to perform. Spending the time and using empathy to understand why they act as they do will pay dividends. It is unlikely that community groups and organizations are deliberately setting out to close an operation down. Using empathy to find a path that meets both their needs and the needs of the unit can pay dividends. It is unlikely that customers really want to skip from supplier to supplier. It is unlikely that suppliers are not trying to build a mutually supportive long-standing relationship with an operation. Again, it often takes an open mind and the right approach to find common ground.

All of this is hard work and thoughtful work. It defines the job of all effective leaders. They recognize all the groups that have to be led and they put in the hard work to get all the constituencies on the same side. It will be a case of building an integrated model of the business and how it fits with all the elements – and for that we can come to the power of thinking about leaders as integrative thinkers.

Chapter Nine

KNOW YOURSELF;
UNDERSTAND OTHERS

Throughout this book I have developed and explained a model of integrative leadership, starting with three self-contained models and then breaking out the nine individual elements within them to show how they interrelate and support one another. Throughout this exposition I have not referred to any particular traits, attributes, or skills, other than a willingness to think hard, motivation to make a difference, and the courage to try. I am sure, though, that the thoughtful leader and careful reader will have picked out several instances where special skills would be helpful or even critical. For instance, it is undoubtedly extremely helpful to have strategic skills and a strategy mindset. The effective leader who can't find a winning strategy can cause the organization to fail or to struggle to stay alive. I believe that people in that kind of situation will still have the personal satisfaction of struggling for a good cause with great values and the personal opportunity to grow. For the emotional health of the people in the organization, it is likely better to be a good leader who is a bad strategist than a good strategist but a bad leader. Much more desirable, of course, is to be good at both.

Other skills are useful in doing the work of the leader. It is useful to have some skill in organization design. There are a lot of productive techniques one can learn that help build an effective team, although much of that work is done by focusing on being an effective leader. It is also useful to have communication skills, having a way with words to articulate the vision and the persuasive power to align and motivate. It is helpful to be comfortable speaking in public and to be an empathetic listener. To be able to live consistently and without compromise according to the values at the core of the leadership message, it is critical to have a moral compass and an awareness of the powerful hidden messages sent by unconscious behaviors and actions.

Beneath all of these particular skills, though, is one fundamental idea. Leadership is an activity that calls on all of our logical and emotional resources and an appreciation of the interconnectedness of the emotional and the logical. It has been said that we have learned more about how the brain functions in the last 10 years than in the last 100 or more. Dr. Ellen Langer, a famous psychology professor at Harvard University, devised a number of creative and original experiments to show how our minds and bodies interact. Just calling an activity "exercise" rather than "work" produces the physiological changes to the body associated with exercise. Calling something "play" instead of "work" produces feelings of happiness. She has produced hundreds of scholarly articles, and her fascinating insights are captured for the general reader in *Mindfulness* and in *Counterclockwise: Mindful Health and the Power of Possibility*.

We are complex creatures. In *How We Decide*, Jonah Lehrer, a Rhodes scholar and writer with an interest in neuroscience, relates some of the findings from that science. It seems that the idea of the rational person who acts and makes decisions purely on logic and facts is not a good representation of what we as humans actually do. Sometimes the emotional side makes the decision, with the logical side left to do the post facto rationalization. Sometimes the logical side predominates while the emotional side acts as the quality check. We are a complex and endlessly interesting bundle of emotion and logic, and we make decisions based on all of our senses. This is an important idea for the leader seeking to understand how to influence others and an equally important idea for the leader who has to understand him or herself in order to function effectively. In the end, leaders are trying to get people to follow their direction with energy and conviction. Sheena Iyengar's brilliant book *The Art of Choosing* gives the thoughtful leader concepts and frameworks to consider when thinking about how to induce people to choose to become energized followers.

One of the more popular ideas about leadership and the competence of leaders comes from Daniel Goleman, whose "What Makes a Leader?" in a 1998 issue of the *Harvard Business Review* brought academic psychology into the center of leadership thinking. Psychologists had always been aware of an idea called emotional intelligence, or EQ, which refers to a special kind of intelligence quite distinct from the ideas of cognitive or intellectual intelligence. EQ is the ability to sense other people's emotions and to act in a way that makes use of that knowledge. It is also the ability to sense the emotions lying beneath the surface in our own minds and exert some control over the impact of those emotions on our own behavior. Kahneman and Tversky, my inspirations for this book, warn that we can never be in complete control of these impacts. But they would also agree that by "thinking slow" we can have some control over their influences on our words and actions. I believe that the best time to "think slow" is before that moment when we have to act fast.

Preparing to lead, preparing to become a leader, is a matter of harnessing these ideas to your advantage, as will be demonstrated in the following sections dealing with assessing the situation, building on your strengths, and becoming a more authentic leader.

Assessing the Situation: Understanding Others

Anyone in a leadership position or contemplating a leadership position will immediately think about the people who have to be led. As demonstrated in chapter 7, "The Dynamics of Leadership," the circle of people to be led can be quite large. Although some will clearly be more critical to the effort, there will be many potential derailers and many whose support will be influential. Assessing the situation should call on both the intellectual and the emotional capabilities of the leader.

The intellectual side will identify the particular resources and talents, limitations and shortcomings, of the people to be led. It will calculate the cost and benefit to each party if the leadership initiative is successful. The intellectual side will naturally identify who needs to approve or provide resources to move anything along. There may be budget implications; the thoughtful leader will have identified whose budget will look better and whose budgets will look worse if a particular course of action is taken. The thoughtful leader will assess whether it will be a case of short-term pain for long-term gain or a win-win for all parties. Another concern is whether the idea will help other leaders move their agenda along or will delay or compromise them.

I find that most people, if pressed, can work through all these logical connections and more. I also find that few people think it through as systematically as they could, and I would encourage everyone to be more thoughtful. When Issy Sharp was developing his business philosophy for Four Seasons, building a service culture from the people up, and investing in people, not physical assets, his intellectual side encountered the logical arguments. Most jobs in the hotel industry are fairly basic and generally considered unskilled or semi-skilled. In the developed world, the jobs are usually in the lower wage category. The intellectual side would say that the people doing these jobs have limited capacity to grow. It might argue that the more talented people in those positions would be looking for better jobs. The turnover of the most qualified would be high. And money spent on the ones who can't find a better job would be wasted. But as Issy traveled around his properties, he met many fine people doing this work. Rather than high turnover, he found that the very best people had been on the job for years or even decades. His intellectual assessment could have been what led to the Four Seasons approach. But he could also do an emotional assessment. He could have felt that these were fine people who should not be treated the way they sometimes were. He could have believed, even if he not been able to prove, that if they were treated better they would perform better. They would not take the training and move on. They would not abuse the opportunity to take an initiative. It's both an intellectual and emotional assessment that leads to a particular course of action.

It is tempting to say that, from a leadership perspective, the emotional assessment is more important. It may or may not be more so, but it is certainly equally important. Bound in the work of Iyengar and the writing of Lehrer is the importance of recognizing the role of the emotional. Many of those who should be influenced by logic and reason to support a well-thought-out idea may still oppose it. Many, who have nothing to gain and could have something to lose, will end up supporting it. The leader's ability to hit the right emotional chord is often the key to creating energized followers or energized opponents. When I was responsible for the George Weston Bakeries business, we closed a well-designed and well-equipped bakery in a very good market with a very highly paid workforce that was struggling while we continued to operate a number of very old and underequipped bakeries that were thriving. The workers in the well-equipped bakery had become, over the years, so angry at management that they behaved in a way that caused them to lose their highly paid jobs, whereas in the other bakeries, the workers were prepared to work with management to continue an effective operation. The view that people are motivated mostly by money just does not fit my experience. The emotional connection to – or distance from – the work can be critical. And leadership plays a big part in making that happen.

But how do we know what people are feeling? It is usually relatively easy to identify the rational arguments for and against a particular line of action. Goleman brought to this daily management task the EQ tools of psychology. Sometimes people will be very candid and open about how they feel about an initiative or course of action. More often their support or opposition will be based on a set of feelings that they may not recognize and will do everything to conceal. In fact, the thoughtful leader will be suspicious about the stated intellectual response as it may (and in my experience is more likely to) hide the real reason.

In his 1998 article, the skills that Goleman identified for this task are empathy (which he now calls social awareness) and social skill (which he now calls the ability to manage relationships). Empathy can be defined as the ability to sense and assess what other people are feeling when they won't tell you and when they may actively try to hide their feelings from you. Social skill is defined as the ability to work with the group's emotions to motivate movement toward the leader's objective.

In his groundbreaking research, he worked through thousands of performance assessment reports. He was trying to discover why some people are seen as having leadership potential and others are not. His research was replicated in a study at my university, the University of Toronto, by Professor Stephane Cote. Professor Cote administered an EQ test to incoming freshmen. As part of his class he had the same students working in small groups. At the end of the group assignment, he asked groups to identify the person or persons who had become the natural leader. His findings confirmed those of Goleman. Those who scored highest in empathy and social awareness were the ones identified by their classmates as the natural leaders. It was not the extroverts who had the most to say, nor the best students. It was not even those who had run for and been successful in gaining positions in student government. It was not related to gender or ethnicity. The people whom others wanted to follow were those they felt "understood" them. I have heard politicians make the same point. People want their elected leaders to be people who understand them, people who "know who I am as a person."

The good news about emotional intelligence is that it is a learned skill. It is not easy to learn but it is learnable. All it takes is a commitment to paying attention, what Ellen Langer would call "mindfulness." All it takes is a lifetime of puzzling about why people do what they do and how one could induce them to do something different. There are many books to learn from. Goleman himself has published at least five, of which *Leadership: The Power of Emotional Intelligence* is a good compendium. When asked I also tell my students to read great literature. Great literature becomes great over time because it gives us an insight into human behavior. Why people do what they do and how they could be induced to do something different is the central theme of perhaps all great writers, including Shakespeare, the greatest writer in the Western tradition.

Of course none of this is a mystery to anyone who has tried to lead thoughtfully. None of this is a mystery to anyone who has sat in a meeting wanting to intervene but holding back because of concerns about the emotions that might be triggered if a different idea is thrown into the mix. It is no mystery to anyone who has worked at "leading up": leading the boss or the board or the management group to follow a desired course of action. When anyone ambitious is in the presence of the boss, the empathy radar goes up and every movement and voice tone is noted and considered. Too often though, I see people leading their own teams with far less attention to the emotional interplay, far less sensitivity to how to tap into the positive emotions and steer clear of the negative. The empathy radar is put away. Too often I see people ignoring the emotional reaction to their good intentions when something is being blocked by a support group or peer group. Too often I hear that the problem is one of "getting the incentives right," as if everyone responded only to rational stimuli.

Perhaps a story might illustrate the point.

In 2001, Dr. Peter Pronovost, a doctor at Johns Hopkins Hospital in Baltimore, developed a checklist of the steps needed to avoid infections when a line is inserted into a patient. To his surprise, the simple checklist produced astounding results. Infection rates went down from about 10 percent to nearly zero. He expanded his idea to other processes and procedures in the intensive care units and got similar results. Today, the World Health Organization (WHO) recognizes the medical . checklist, and the surgical checklist in particular, as the most significant improvement in medical care in decades. It measurably decreases errors and adverse events and increases teamwork and collaboration. The intellectual argument for using checklists is irrefutable. And yet today, years after the results have been seen and replicated over and over, it remains difficult to implement the system in many hospitals. The leadership problem is not to sell the logic; it is to overcome the emotion. Many doctors would say that they are doing all the same things anyway, that they have a way of doing things that works and should not be interrupted. Some say that they need to spend their time on patient care and not on paperwork.

In 2007 and 2008, Dr. Bryce Taylor, who was, among his many jobs, surgeon-in-chief at the University Health Network in Toronto, was part of a world study on the use of a 19-item surgical checklist at eight hospitals around the world, four in the developed world and four in the developing world. The results were dramatic and irrefutable. The rate of death declined from 1.5 percent to 0.8% after the checklist was introduced. Inpatient complications declined from 11 percent to 7 percent. When we consider the number of people undergoing surgery around the world at any one time, these numbers are staggering. Millions of lives could be saved. Billions of dollars could be saved.

Dr. Taylor participated in the study with some skepticism. He believed that surgery at his hospital was already well done. By the end of the study he was convinced. His surgical teams were good, but the surgical checklist would make them better. He brought the idea back to his own hospital. Who better than the surgeon-in-chief to be the champion? The initial reception was less than enthusiastic. Surgeons and anesthetists already had their own routines, which they considered safe and thorough. They were busy and did not have the time. It just seemed like paperwork.

These were all great arguments to support a decision that the emotional part of their brains had already made. As scientists they should have been overwhelmed by the data and changed immediately. But as humans they had strong emotional reactions that led to an understandably irrational decision. Surgeons are people too! With that assessment, Dr. Taylor could develop a more thoughtful way to lead the change than simply to rely on the data and impose the system. Surgeons needed to *own* the checklist. He let them develop their own modified version. They needed to be reminded, so for several months he attended every 7 a.m. surgical meeting. They needed to be validated, so he did a follow-up study to show that the checklist was making a difference. They needed to make it just "one of the things that we always do," so he identified outliers and resisters and dealt with them individually. They still needed to be reminded, so he gave the person in the operating room with the least amount of formal power the task of ensuring the checklist was used each and every time. It takes repetition to create a habit.

The surgical checklist is now firmly implanted in the University Health Network in Toronto. Follow-up surveys show that 100 percent of nurses are firmly committed. Only 80 percent of doctors are as committed. With the processes in place, the 20 percent who are less committed are unlikely to make much headway in going back to the old ways. And if everyone is doing it, it becomes socially unacceptable to be the outlier.

Every successful leader I have spoken to or listened to is very thoughtful and introspective about how they assessed the situation and how they went about it. As I mentioned at the beginning of the book, I had the good fortune to be at the Rotman School when we had a virtual parade of leaders from around the world tell their story. With the lens of integrative thinking they shared their insight into their thoughts at critical times. To a person, they were as tuned into the emotional as the logical when they considered how they would lead.

Know Yourself: Capabilities and Emotions

One of the best – and worst – things about leadership is that it is all about you. If you are able to "get someone else to do something that you want done because he wants to do it," to use another Eisenhower quote, you have led. If you can't, you have not. You don't need to go any further. The report card is simple. You lead and they follow, or you lead and they choose to go another way. If it worked, you led. If it did not work, you were not an effective leader. If it worked, congratulate yourself. If it did not, don't blame anyone else. If the boss doesn't support your idea, you did not lead the boss effectively. If the people in the meeting don't pick up on your idea, you did not find a way to present the idea and yourself in a persuasive or convincing way. If it worked, analyze what you did and why it worked so that you have tools to use the next time. If it did not work, analyze the situation and how you proceeded and see what can be changed for the next time.

The idea of self-awareness and its power and influence on a person's performance is well known. From my early adulthood I often heard about "knowing yourself." Strength and weakness charts and self-help books have been around for decades. Some concentrate on identifying weaknesses that could be career derailers and working on them. Some concentrate on identifying strengths that should be leveraged. Virtually every large organization puts their people through some kind of annual performance evaluation that aims to identify the strengths and the "areas for improvement," to use the common jargon.

It is useful for any leader to have a keen appreciation of the skills and capabilities that they bring to any task. When I became president of George Weston North American Bakeries, I never forgot that being president was my first job in the bakery industry. If I was going to contribute, it would not be by having brilliant ideas about how to operate the ovens. In contrast, when people with a lifetime of experience in an industry take on a job, it is expected and normal to immediately set to work fixing the operations. I knew I had strategic and organizational development skills from my many years as a strategy consultant to a variety of industries. I could see things at a conceptual level that could not be seen by the people who were so immersed in the detail that they had lost perspective. I knew I had the ability to relate to many different kinds of people from many years of playing team sports and from summer jobs in factories and warehouses. I was not tainted by decades of labor/management disagreements. I knew that I was very comfortable on my feet making a presentation to small or large groups, in formal and informal settings.

I could go on. But this is not a book about me or how I did things. The point is that everyone comes into any job or situation with strengths and weaknesses, blind spots and perceptive insights. The trick is to be aware of, and work with, the strengths while being mindful of the traps that are hidden by your weaknesses.

This level of self-awareness is useful and necessary but is not sufficient for the rounded assessment needed to be an effective leader. It needs to be supplemented by the ideas of self-awareness and self-management – the other half of Goleman's emotional intelligence framework. The self-awareness idea is that we are all, to a very large extent, captured by emotions. Our emotions will blind us to what may be obvious to others, or it may persuade us that we have seen something that simply is not there. Kahneman and Tversky did study after study and made observation after observation about this phenomena. In addition to demonstrating how our emotions affect our actions – which is disconcerting enough – they were also able to demonstrate how easily our emotions can be triggered and, once triggered, how immediately they affect our behavior: giving someone a paragraph to read that contains words like "spring" and "fresh" translates into that same person walking more quickly. Emotions can be triggered that make us more altruistic or more selfish, more forgiving or more vindictive, more sexist or racist or more inclusive.

It requires a certain level of humility to accept that this could be me. Most of us, perhaps, believe that we can rise above it, that our actions are rational and well founded, not the product of our emotions. And yet the evidence from decades of studies shows that no one is immune. For the leader, this knowledge is critical because it leads to what Goleman called self-management, the ability to act in accordance with what the situation demands rather than with the pull of our emotions. Goleman's self-management idea is a specific manifestation of Kahneman and Tversky's thinking slow idea. Self-managing people are more likely to think before acting, to exercise some self-censorship before speaking. Suppose someone has said or done something that makes you angry. Is anger the right response? Will it get you farther down the path that you want to lead? Or is there a more appropriate response? "Let cooler heads prevail" is a common way of expressing this idea, and the image portrayed in popular media – film and television – invariably shows the hero as the one who is cool under fire.

All of these ideas will flash through the brain of someone sitting in a meeting trying to decide whether to intervene. That person will be aware of their own strengths and shortcomings in relation to the topic at hand. Do they have relevant experience or specialized knowledge that gives them a unique perspective? Will their experience and knowledge be seen as relevant and useful by others in the meeting? Do they have the communication skills to express their point of view in this setting or do they need to wait for a quieter moment or an opportunity to have a one-on-one with someone of influence? The objective factors line up in their mind. But they are less than half of the factors that will influence the intervention. There are anxieties about how people will react and what they will think, at that time and in other settings. The desire to intervene might be triggered by anger at the way some people are conducting themselves. The intervention may be more about putting someone down or building someone up than the objective facts of the situation.

The EQ hypothesis is that if we are aware of how hidden emotions influence our behavior in the moment, we are more likely to be able to regulate our actions against a bigger agenda that goes beyond the moment. Kahneman would say that there are times when we have to think slow to control the impulsiveness of our thinking fast reflex. Thoughtful leaders will have a clear picture of the overall message they want to deliver. That clear picture will inform a thoughtful response, which will come across as spontaneous. The president of a very large media company told me once that when he took the job, he kept his eye out for opportunities to show his leadership. With his eyes open he reacted to some events that he might, without that lens, have left for someone else. The person sitting in the meeting might be the boss who knows the answer but sits quietly to see how the team performs, knowing that an intervention will shut off the discussion. Or the person in the meeting may be a peer who needs to demonstrate a higher level of involvement in order to have influence later on. The thoughtful leader has a thoughtful agenda. The agenda is a vehicle for guiding the self-regulated actions.

Know Yourself: Authenticity

In 2003, Bill George wrote *The Authentic Leader: Rediscovering the Secrets to Creating Lasting Value*. Although authenticity had been discussed and researched in academic circles for years, it was not part of the popular leadership development material. By 2015, Herminia Ibarra, one of the seminal thinkers on leadership, declared that "authenticity has become the gold standard for leadership." The authenticity idea is a powerful one. Put simply, it states that if a person is perceived as authentic, that person is likely to be trusted. And if that person is trusted, then they are likely to be believed. And if they are believed, the chances of getting acceptance of their ideas about visions, values, strategy, clarity, and so on are much enhanced. But what is authenticity?

When I ask people why they are doing their job, they invariably respond with some form of the organization's objectives. They are running this clinic to provide excellent health care to this community. They are the principal of this school to ensure that these children get the best possible foundation for the rest of their lives. They are running this department, or division, or company to deliver these products or services to customers, to gain this market share, and to provide these returns to investors. These are all worthwhile purposes. And they need to be kept front and center in your mind because they will form the basis for other people's judgments about whether you are succeeding. Think of them as the objectives that you have to live up to in order to keep your job. But do these kinds of statements really reflect why you are doing your job?

Are you running the clinic because this is a good community to raise a family, the job pays well, the colleagues are pleasant, and the hours reasonable? Are you the principal of this school because successful performance will put you in line to be a superintendent? Are you running the department, division, or company as a steppingstone to something else? These are probably the real answers to the question of why you are doing the job. But they are seldom the answers that I get. These are the real questions that everyone in an organization discusses about anyone in a leadership position. What is their "real" agenda? How long will they be there? How is that "real" agenda shaping the way that they do things, the decisions that they make, and the people they spend time with? I know from experience as a director and as a CEO that these questions are regularly discussed about the people in the company. Are they here for the long term? What are their real career/life goals? The consensus answer to these questions – usually reached without including the person who is the subject of them – forms the background for assessing the authenticity of the leader and, through that, the leader's credibility and, through that, the leader's ability to get their message across.

Bill George is the former chairman and CEO of Medtronic and, for more than a decade, a professor of management practice at the Harvard Business School. His books are excellent discourses on the subject of authenticity. In George's view, leadership begins and ends with authenticity. His argument resonates with my view that leadership is not about style or traits or attributes but is about what you do with who you are. My integrated model can help with what you do, but each individual has to figure out who they are. In *True North*, the author works through a number of self-reflection exercises to help people find their authentic self, to find out what truly motivates them and how their work life integrates with their whole life.

George believes that truly authentic leaders desire to serve others through their leadership. I wish this were true. I believe that the desire to lead comes from many motivations. The trick is to find the one that fits you. In fact, I believe that one of the impediments to authenticity as a leader is a belief that the only worthy purpose is the altruistic one. That works if it is true. But it often is not. I also believe that people are generous and understanding about what may be perceived as a more selfish purpose. No one begrudges the person who pushes for the bigger job because the money is better or the working conditions are better or because it is a steppingstone to a higher goal. What people don't like is to be told that a leader's motivation is about service, dedication to the cause, and commitment to the group if it is not. George also believes that there is one true authentic "you" and when you find it you have to be true to it. Ibarra believes that we have several authentic "yous," and we need to find the one that is most appropriate for the situation. I lean toward Ibarra but caution about getting too far from the core "you."

Authenticity is power for anyone who wants to lead. People have to believe that they can trust the leader. They have to believe that they know "where you are coming from," to use a popular phrase. Too often aspiring leaders leave too much doubt about where they are coming from because they don't want to expose their selfish reasons for leading. This is understandable but eventually self-defeating. It is far better to find a productive way to express your true personal purpose so that whatever you say after is credible. You can be trusted even if you are not liked.

What would authenticity look like, and how does personal purpose intersect with the purpose of the organization or initiative being led? Let's go back to the examples from the start of this section. What would be wrong with the clinic manager saying, "I really like this community while my kids are growing up and I really like working with all of you, so I am here to do everything that I can to serve the community so that the future of the clinic is secured"? Personal and corporate purpose are combined authentically. What would be wrong with the principal saying, "I am not sure how long I will be here because I plan to apply for a superintendent position one of these days, so I want to work with you to make this the best school that it can possibly be"? Personal and corporate purpose are combined authentically. What would be wrong with the department head saying, "I am really hoping that we can break through to a higher level of performance so that each of us who wants to be promoted, including me, will have a better chance and so that all who want to stay with the division will have better jobs and more money"? Personal and corporate purpose are combined authentically.

Leadership as Creative Problem Solving

Under the heading of "know yourself; understand others," I have presented three fundamental ideas which can be thought of as the building blocks to becoming a thoughtful leader. The first idea uses the empathy and social skills of emotional intelligence – ideas that Goleman now calls social awareness and the ability to manage relationships – to understand others. Those ideas are fundamental to thinking through how to get people aligned, to understanding motivation, to finding the right way to harness the power of involvement. The second idea uses the self-awareness and self-regulation skills of emotional intelligence to temper our "fast thinking" impulses into a more thoughtful "slow thinking" approach, which is more likely to be consistent and targeted. It is also the skill that is called on to be consistently true to the espoused values of the group. The third idea is authenticity, which requires leaders to come to grips with why they are taking on the difficult mantle of leadership in order to harness the power of being seen as credible. In presenting these ideas, I pointed out that the ideas require an assessment and assimilation of the logical facts of the situation with the emotions that are always at play.

How do these ideas come together?

I believe that whenever we are faced with a task to be achieved, our minds automatically move to three pre-activity assessments. The first is that we need to understand why we are taking on the task. The second is that we think about the situation – the environmental constraints and opportunities. The third is that we assess the resources we have to accomplish the task.

As shown in the chart in Figure 9.1, this process maps to the three fundamental skills that underpin any leader. Imagine being handed some kind of leadership task. It could be promotion to a new position. It could be responsibility for a project team. It could be taking the lead on the implementation of a new initiative. For most people, their first thought is to get clarity on what is expected and by when. I call this the objective or corporate purpose. At the same time, I believe that most people will start thinking about what it means for them. Is this an opportunity that could lead to a better future? Does the new assignment open doors? Does it lead to more security or reward? Will it require you to act in a way that is inconsistent with the way that you comfortably act? Will it require you to be more collaborative when you are more comfortable being self-reliant? Will it require you to be more authoritarian when you are more comfortable being a consensus builder? The purpose box in the chart maps to these two ways of thinking about a leadership challenge or opportunity. On one side is the objective result to be delivered. On the other are the personal goals that may be attainable and the personal challenges that may have to be overcome. The authenticity argument suggests that thinking through the personal is as important as getting clarity on the objective. Failure to be clear on the personal creates many opportunities to wander thoughtlessly into actions and behaviors that will be seen as inauthentic. And perceived inauthenticity can be a big drag on leadership effectiveness.

The next two boxes in the chart address the situation assessment, including an assessment of the resources available to accomplish the task. In a leadership situation, the situation assessment is primarily focused on who has to be led. And that assessment should cover both the hard facts and the emotional landscape. The hard facts would include the particular skills, aptitudes, and availability of the people involved – the hard-headed assessment of the available talent. The emotional landscape is assessed with Goleman's empathy and social awareness skills.

Figure 9.1. Becoming a more effective leader

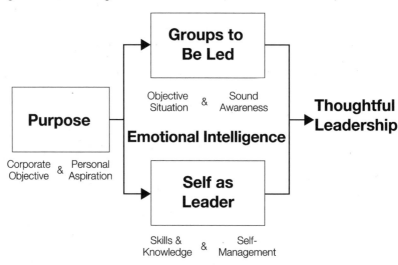

How will the people to be led feel about you as a leader? How do they feel about being part of your initiative? How will they feel about the success of the project, and how do they feel about the prospect of you being successful? These are questions that are seldom asked and, if they are, are seldom answered truthfully. We all hide our feelings. These are the kinds of answers that are only gleaned through the lens of emotional intelligence – picking up clues, looking for nuances, watching body language. There are good reasons why high emotional intelligence is associated with effective leaders.

The next box on the chart is an assessment of the resources that you have to bring to bear on the project. In the case of a leadership situation, there is only one resource that matters and that is you. If it works, pat yourself on the back. If it does not, consider what you learned. Again you can do the self-assessment from a logical and an emotional perspective. Logically you can ask what hard skills you bring to the task. Do you have some expertise in the subject matter? Do you have strategy or planning skills that will be useful? Are you more or less "expert" in the topic compared to the rest of the team? And then comes the hard emotional assessment. How do you feel about the task? Do you worry that it may be beyond your capabilities? Will your team members include people with whom you have difficulty working? Are there team members that you simply do not like? Will you have to work with support groups that have never appeared very supportive? Are you concerned about the people to whom you will be reporting? Self-awareness is critical because of its connection to self-regulation. Thinking slow to be aware of your emotional state is the precursor to being able to control and regulate your emotions in a "thinking fast" situation. Effective leaders are aware that they need to act in a way that is productive for what they are trying to achieve.

Authenticity, social awareness, and self-regulation prepare anyone to be a more effective leader.

Chapter Ten

FINAL THOUGHTS

This book set out to help you learn to be a better leader by being more thoughtful about what leadership is and how it is practiced. It set out to help people who are already effective as leaders to become even better by giving them a framework for understanding what they are actually doing that makes them so effective so they can repeat their effectiveness and become even better leaders in the future. It sets out to encourage anyone with a good idea – especially one that will make the world a better place – to step up and give it a try. It sets out to persuade anyone in a position of influence that leadership can be taught and that producing more and better leaders will be good for their organization. Leaders develop leaders.

Leadership is such an interesting topic because it is difficult but doable. It can be done brilliantly to great and memorable effect. It can be done well and produce good work and fulfilled people. And it can be done poorly and produce failures and bitterness. I believe that almost anyone who is motivated can do it reasonably well and that there is no reason to accept poor leadership. On the other hand, between reasonably well done and brilliant is a lifetime journey of learning, exploration, and thoughtful experience. Socrates is reputed to have said that "the unexamined life is not worth living." I am no Socrates, but I would say that the unexamined experiences of a leader are a treasure that would be a tragedy to leave unexplored.

At the same time, I recognize that because leadership is hard and can be personally risky, it is not for everyone. Too often I have seen people take the promotion because it is offered, because there is more money, or because it is a point of pride with family and friends. If the truth were told, they do not want the position. They would rather be the salesman than the district manager, the bond trader than the group head. They would rather be the clinician than the medical director, the teacher than the principal. The world would be a better place if they turned down the promotion. The world would be a better place if they stayed in a situation that gave them personal satisfaction rather than venture into a place that requires what might be, for them, unnatural acts. In my experience it is the people who really don't want to lead who do it badly. And when they do it badly they make themselves and the people around them very unhappy. A large part of what drives me to continue to teach leadership and to learn more about it is to reduce the number of people out there who inadvertently make people unhappy. The misery that bad leaders create multiplies. Sending people home and into their communities every day feeling unfulfilled, frustrated, belittled, and unable to make a productive contribution can lead to unhappy families and divided communities. I am always happy when former students get in touch with stories of their own leadership success. But as they talk, my mind will wander to the thousands of other people who will be affected by what they do. Leadership makes a big difference in our society.

Leadership is hard but it is doable. Leadership is risky but it is rewarding. Some people are pessimistic about the state of leadership today, but I am not; I see it all around me and I see the eagerness of my students to learn how to be better, whether they are in MBA programs developing their own skills or with their work colleagues making their organizations better places. When I started, many people in the class were still in the command and control mindset with an image that they could soon climb the corporate ladder and start bossing. It was a revelation to lay out the ideas of John Kotter, about the need to be visionary, to be a salesperson for the vision, and to focus on motivation not compliance. Today this is no longer an issue or even a topic. Today's students fully embrace the idea that to lead is to bring out the best in people.

Today's students fully accept the idea that leaders go beyond compliance to motivation and beyond that to engagement.

The idea of integrating nine different elements in the context of leading up, down, and around may seem daunting, but I have seen over and over how easily and naturally it can be done by students from all kinds of occupations. Over the last year alone I have taught people from many different kinds of businesses, from several continents, school principals and superintendents, nurse and clinic managers in large teaching hospitals, bankers and brokers, public service workers and police officers, lawyers and Children's Aid workers. In my MBA classes are people from all parts of the world with their own diverse experiences. They all are able to pick up the ideas and put them to work. They seldom have difficulty filling in all nine boxes and having them fit and support each other. In practice, people generally find that the internal logic of the framework is so powerful that filling in one box naturally leads to the box beside it.

In fact, once one becomes familiar with what I've called the 9Box framework, opportunities to use it as a thoughtful approach to any number of human situations will become apparent. For example, consider yourself preparing to meet a new customer. Or consider how you might approach a customer when your organization is trying to make the transition from transactional selling to the development of a deeper relationship. The meeting will include some scripted moments and some critical moments that will happen spontaneously. The idea of using "thinking slow" time to prepare for the "thinking fast" unscripted time works well with the 9Box framework. The meeting will start down the middle column with some way of describing the vision for the relationship and considerable time spent aligning – selling that vision – while highlighting all the elements of the relationship that should be motivational to the customer. It is likely that next the conversation will shift to the managing column, showing the plan for serving the customer's needs, including who will do the work and how the results will be assessed and measured. Then the conversation can switch to the right-hand side of the chart – setting out the values that will underlie the relationship (integrity, transparency, and so on) and offering clarity on how far the relationship will reach – and will conclude by inquiring how the customer wants to be involved. The premise is that being a thoughtful leader will help guide the reaction to the unexpected moment. Time spent thinking through the 9Box framework is great preparation for a consistent response that is likely to be "on message" with the overall approach.

I often think about the framework in a fundraising situation. Fundraisers are always selling – seeking alignment with – some lofty purpose, a vision. They are tuned to the various ways that people can be motivated to support that vision. Fundraisers are likely to move from the middle column to the right, emphasizing the values that underlie the purpose with clarity on what can be expected and offering opportunities for greater and more personal involvement. The close usually requires some time spent on the left side of the framework, showing how the money will be carefully spent by people who know what they are doing with appropriate controls in place.

These are two concrete examples, but opportunities abound. I had one student report to me how he used the framework to persuade a landlord to lease space for his unconventional business in a prestigious office tower. I have had other students report how they used the framework to prepare for a job interview. Others tell me that they keep a picture of the 9Box on the wall and use it to assess whether they should support project ideas being pitched to them by members of their team. Many use it as a diagnostic tool when a project or even a part of their operation is not doing or performing well.

As I said at the beginning, this book will help you learn to be a better leader by being more thoughtful about what leadership is, how you are expressing it in your daily life, and how you exercise it when necessary. As these examples demonstrate, being thoughtful beforehand is a good guide to being effective in the moment. You will notice as well that, though I gave a few examples from my own life, it is not in any way a book about how I led. It is the book that I wish had been there when I was leading. I know that all of you can do a much better job and that your work will make the world a better place. I wish you well in your own leadership journey.

ACKNOWLEDGMENTS

When I started this project it did not seem so hard. I had been teaching the material in a leadership course for several years. The ideas, their sequence, and their interrelationship were clear in my head. I had many illustrative stories that I had used in class or had learned from my students. What could be so difficult? As it turns out, this may have been the most difficult thing that I have ever done. And it could not have been done without the help of many people. I would like to acknowledge just a few.

I will start with my wonderful colleague, the extraordinary teacher and scholar Professor Tiziana Casciaro. We taught the first-year leadership course in the MBA program together. Professor Casciaro brought the material that she had used teaching a course with the same name at Harvard Business School. I brought the 9Box framework I had been working out as I taught the leadership course to the Executive MBA classes. Tiziana saw the value and the originality of the framework but would only include it if I wrote up a teaching note with all the appropriate acknowledgments and references. This was my first attempt to nail the ideas down and make them more concrete.

It might have ended there were it not for the intervention of Karen Christiansen, the incomparable editor-in-chief of *Rotman Management*, the magazine that she created and has nurtured into one of the most important magazines bridging the divide between management academics and those who practice the art. Karen read that initial teaching note and, along with her colleague Steve Arenburg, who is on top of every new book and new idea in the business press, urged and encouraged me to turn it into a book.

Many of my students asked when I was going to turn my ideas into a book. Two in particular did not let the idea drop after they graduated. Alicia Hare and Sarbjit Raj insisted that I had a responsibility to put my ideas out there for the benefit of all those people who would never be able to attend a class or take the full course. Even as they suffered through early drafts, they found the nicest possible ways to say "this isn't really good enough" and "this is not the course that you teach." And then every few months they would be back to me asking for the state of the next draft.

I received invaluable assistance and inspiration from my friend, former boss, and colleague Roger Martin. He set a great example with his own literary output, and his intellectual contribution is cited in the book. Despite being one of the busiest people on the planet, he took the time to read early drafts and had the courtesy of offering unsparing criticisms and exhortations to "do it right" and "make it a book you will be proud of." I hope that I have come close to his expectations.

In the last five years I have been privileged to work alongside Rose Patten co-directing a one-week Executive Leadership Program. Rose has had a lifetime of working with leaders at all levels as a mentor, advisor, developer, and appointer. Her experience is as deep as her wisdom. She helped me when she did not even know it – or perhaps she did. In particular, she was invaluable in making me see where my ideas fit into a constellation of other useful approaches. She was always ready to read another draft and offer insights and contributions that were always to the point. I am pleased to say that I will not be asking her to spend another summer with another draft.

I should also acknowledge my friend Dr. Bryce Taylor. In addition to being featured in chapter 8 as a truly effective leader, he read and made voluminous notes on an early draft. He also was an inspiration when his own book, *Effective Medical Leadership*, was published and I realized that he had written it while holding down an important, stressful, and very busy job. If he could do all that, I needed to stop complaining and get to it.

Over the 17 years that I have been teaching my course on leadership at the Rotman School, I have given my students one and only one final assignment. At the end of the course I ask the students to write me a short story about an experience in their own life where they were the leader or observed a leader. I ask them to tell me about the situation and whether the leadership was successful or not. If it was successful, they were to use the course framework to explain why. If it was unsuccessful, they were to use the same framework to explain what was missing and to tell me whether it provided insight into how the problems could have been avoided. I have read thousands of these stories and never get tired of them. The stories gave me confidence that the framework could be usefully applied in all kinds of situations and that it was not culturally specific. Most of the stories are set in North America, but I have some from Europe, China, India, Africa, and Latin America. I have stories from the public and private sectors, from for-profits and not-for-profits, from social groups and sports teams. While the tactics differ by culture and setting, the job of the leader remains the same. People want to know that their work has purpose, that they can make a meaningful contribution, and that someone is paying attention to the work they do. The principles of leadership are universal.

To Daniela Pizarro, my friend, executive assistant, and teaching assistant of so many years, I can only say "it is finally finished." Daniela wanted me to get this finished before she returned to Chile. I didn't quite make it, but thank you for all your help and encouragement.

Finally let me thank Jennifer DiDomenico of University of Toronto Press, who saw the promise of this project and kept it going. She was gentle but persistent in pointing out the flaws and omissions and always made it seem like the finish line was "just around the corner." And then it was.

Anyone and everyone who picks up this book has an idea that will make some part of some organization a little or a lot better. I hope I have given you the courage to try and the skill to succeed. You will make the world a better place for all of us, and that will make it all worthwhile.

REFERENCES

Chapter One

Amos Tversky and Daniel Kahneman have been famous in academic circles and academic journals for decades. In 2011, after receiving his Nobel Prize for their contribution to the field of economics, Kahneman made their work accessible to the public in *Thinking Fast and Slow* (Doubleday Canada, 2011).

Roger Martin began searching for a way to integrate the academic management disciplines from the day that he became dean of the Rotman School of Management in 1998. His thinking and conclusions are captured in *The Opposable Mind: How Successful Leaders Win through Integrative Thinking* (Harvard Business School Publishing, 2007).

Michael Useem writes about several people who face "leadership moments" – some requiring an instant reaction, some with an opportunity for reflection – in *The Leadership Moment* (Crown Publishing, 1999).

Chapter Two

The Eisenhower quote is found in the Eisenhower Presidential Library and is from remarks at the Remarks at the Breakfast Meeting of Republican State Chairmen in Denver, Colorado, September 10, 1955.

A.G. Lafley wrote about how he changed P&G in *The Game-Changer: How You Can Drive Revenue and Profit Growth with Innovation* with Ram Charan (Crown Publishing, 2008). On November 21, 2005, Roger

Martin interviewed him on stage at the Rotman School. Roger probed him on how he handled difficult decisions.

Issy Sharp built the Four Seasons hotel chain from his hometown, Toronto. I am familiar with his early hotels and have stayed in many others around the world. His story is often told in the popular press in his hometown. The first time I heard the whole story from his perspective was when he spoke at the Rotman School in Toronto on April 11, 2002.

K.V. Kamath gave a talk and answered questions about the rise of ICICI Bank at the Rotman School, Toronto, on April 16, 2004.

Piers Handling talked about the tough choices he made in taking the Toronto Film Festival from obscurity to perhaps the most important festival in the industry in a session at the Rotman School, Toronto, on March 7, 2002.

At the Rotman School, Toronto, on March 4, 2003, John Sterman gave a lively and entertaining class about his systems thinking ideas and how they are grounded in the idea that we are all unconscious model builders.

I referred to Daniel Kahneman's *Thinking Fast and Slow* in the previous chapter.

I referred to Roger Martin's *The Opposable Mind* in the previous chapter. The model itself is described in chapter 2, pp. 25–48.

Throughout the book there are many references to Inditex, Zara, and Armancio Ortega. Ortega recently was named the world's wealthiest man, which attracts a good deal of media attention. The articles, case studies, and books that I have reviewed include Pankaj Ghemawat and Jose Luis Nueno, *ZARA: Fast Fashion* (Harvard Business School Publishing, 2003); John R. Wells and Galen Danskin, *Inditex 2012* (Harvard Business School Publishing, 2014); Professor Felipe Caro, *Zara: Staying Fast and Fresh* (case study produced by UCLA Anderson School of Management, 2011); Covadonga O'Shea, *The Man from Zara: The Story of the Genius behind the Inditex Group* (LID Publishing, 2012). Ortega's story is often in the public press: "Ortega Tops Buffett with Zara Fortune," *Bloomberg* magazine, October 2012; "Rosalia Meyer, World's Richest Self-Made Woman, Dies Aged 69," *Guardian*, August

16, 2013; "A Better Business Model," *Financial Times*, June 19, 2014; John Gapper, "American Apparel's Resistance to Fast Fashion Is Futile," *Financial Times*, October 8, 2015. The website of Inditex, the parent company of Zara, provides more detail on how the company provides value beyond profit.

John Kotter's famous article "What Do Leaders Really Do?" first appeared in the *Harvard Business Review* in March 1990.

I referred to Michael Useem's *The Leadership Moment* in the previous chapter.

The Walmart story has been told in many places. Its corporate website leads with its vision of "Saving people money so they can live better." Over the years I have had many students in my classes who work at Walmart and have supplemented the public information with the message they hear directly from the management today. It is from them that I have learned about the very clear focus on "the bottom half" of the economic spectrum.

Simon Sinek has given many popular TED talks. The talk on September 28, 2009, sets out the basic argument. The idea is further developed in the bestselling *Start With Why: How Great Leaders Inspire Everyone to Take Action* (Penguin, 2011).

Peter Drucker is perhaps the world's most prolific writer on management. Many of his best ideas are found in Peter F. Drucker, *The Essential Drucker* (Harper Collins, 2008).

Jack Welch was chairman and CEO of General Electric from 1980 to 2000. When people started to realize that he was not behaving like a traditional big company CEO and that General Electric was not suffering the same fate as other old manufacturing businesses, he became a celebrity CEO. In 1987 he spoke to an overflow crowd of students at the Harvard Business School, and his remarks and responses to questions were captured in a video. Additional material from Jack Welch is from *Jack Welch at GE 1981–2001: The Evolution of a Chief Executive* (Harvard Business Publishing video, 2009).

The "task without a vision" quote has many variants and is said to have been inscribed in stone on a church in Surrey, England, in 1730.

But sometimes the church is in Sussex and sometimes it is 1640. Perhaps it is best left as wise but anonymous.

I picked up Joseph L. Badaracco and Richard R. Ellsworth's *Leadership and the Quest for Integrity* (Harvard Business School Publishing, 1989) while attending my 25-year alumni reunion at the Harvard Business School. The authors built very powerful arguments in support of three different models of leadership. They believed that leaders have to choose one of those models and follow it. The models resonated with my own experience, but I recognized that when I had been most successful I followed all three at the same time. Furthermore, I recognized that there is no contradiction in integrating the three approaches.

The article on goal setting by Gary P. Latham and Edwin A. Locke, "Building a Practically Useful Theory of Goal Setting and Task Motivation: A 35-Year Odyssey," *American Psychologist*, September 2002, is one of the most frequently cited articles in the field of organization behaviour.

Issy Sharp stated his vision and values for the company in a discussion at the Rotman School in April 2002. He has also written about it in *Four Seasons: The Story of a Business Philosophy* (Penguin, 2012). The values statement is repeated in many forms on the corporate website. Four Seasons has also been the subject of several business school cases, including Roger Hallowell and Abby Hansen, *Four Seasons Hotels and Resorts* (Harvard Business School Publishing, 2000), and Roger Hallowell, David Bowen, and Carin-Isabel Knoop, *Four Seasons Goes to Paris: "53 Properties, 24 Countries, 1 Philosophy"* (Harvard Business School Publishing, 2003).

The Google vision is at the top of the corporate website and its values are set out on the same site. The values are also part of *How Google Works* by Eric Schmidt and Jonathan Rosenberg with Alan Eagle (Grand Central Publishing, 2014).

Chapter Three

The thinking behind the remarkable turnaround of P&G in the early years of the millennium is documented in Lafley and Charan, *The*

Game-Changer. The quote "purpose-led and values-driven" is found on p. 11.

The Shafiq Agarwal story is adapted from a student's final paper. Some details have been changed to provide anonymity, but all of the leadership actions are as they were reported.

Chapter Four

The Starbucks story has been told many times in many places. In 2011 *Fortune* magazine named Schultz "Businessperson of the Year," with extensive write-ups on his early history and that of Starbucks. The story is also told in Bill George's *True North* (Wiley, 2007) and is repeated in the November 2014 issue of *Fortune* magazine. Schultz's account of his return to Starbucks to re-energize the vision and then to rebuild the management fundamentals is recounted in Howard Schultz with Joanne Gordon, *Onward: How Starbucks Fought for Its Life without Losing Its Soul* (Rodale, 2011). The anecdote about smelling the cheese is on p. 37; the stuffed animal story is on p. 90. It is interesting to go to a Starbucks today and see the staff put the sandwiches into paper bags before heating so that the coffee aroma is not overwhelmed.

Presidential approval ratings can be found on the websites of the *Washington Post*, Gallup, CBS, and CNN.

The English translation of Fayol's lengthy tome is found as Henri Fayol, *General and Industrial Management* (Pitman, 1949).

The *Economist* on June 4, 2009, revisited the Ford Foundation's famous *Higher Education for Business*, popularly known as the Gordon-Howell Report, as well as the Carnegie Foundation's more measured *The Education of American Businessmen* by Frank Pierson.

There are many variations of the managing cycle idea, often referred to as the functions of management. Some include "leading" as one of the functions. Kotter broke out leading and simplified the management functions as "Plan, Organize, Control" in his 1990 *Harvard Business Review* article, "What Do Leaders Really Do?"

For Jack Welch, the term "grunt" was a compliment meant to refer to the people who do the hard work on the front line as opposed to the critics in the head office removed from the action. It is referred to in a *US News* column by Bill Lane from January 25, 2008.

One of the more famous books about the importance of doing the hard work of managing is Larry Bossidy and Ram Charan, *Execution: The Discipline of Getting Things Done* (Crown Business, 2002).

Over 30 years ago, Peter Drucker was providing wisdom and insight into the practice of management. His "New Templates for Today's Organization" was found in the *Harvard Business Review* in January 1974.

Sharon Vinderine posted her love affair with Starbucks on the *Huffington Post* with "How Starbucks Turned Me Into a Brand Ambassador" on October 1, 2012.

Chapter Five

This famous quote from Antoine de Saint-Exupéry is found on many quotation sites, though I have never found the original source.

The "I Have a Dream" speech was given by Dr. Martin Luther King on August 28, 1963 at the March on Washington and can still be heard on YouTube.

I first found the Mandela image in Adam Kahane's *Solving Tough Problems: An Open Way of Talking, Listening, and Creating New Realities* (Berrett-Koehler, 2004). In 1991 and 1992 Kahane was "loaned" to South Africa to facilitate what was called the Mont Fleur Scenario Exercise to effect the transition to democracy. The story of the adoption of the flamingo image is on pp. 19–33.

I visited Berlin in 2012 and visited many sites that retell the story. The *Telegraph* published its own retelling of the story on the 25th anniversary of the occasion, May 19, 2015.

When Anne Mulcahy stepped down from her role as chairman and CEO of Xerox, she gave many speeches at business schools, which are available on the Internet. Her speeches at Stanford and MIT are especially interesting.

I have been using the case study by Rosabeth Moss Kanter, *Charlotte Beers at Ogilvy and Mather Worldwide (A)* (Harvard Business School

Publishing, May 1995), in my class for many years. Last year a student took the initiative to phone Beers to inquire about the story and found that she was as passionate as ever about the advertising industry and the importance of leadership.

The description of the development of a vision statement for the Body Shop is found in the early chapters of Anita Roddick, *Body and Soul: Profits with Principles – The Amazing Success Story of Anita Roddick and The Body Shop* (Crown, 1991).

Bill George left his position as CEO of Medtronic in 2001 after 10 very successful years to become an educator. His work at Harvard as a professor of practice began to focus on the power of authenticity, and his book *Authentic Leadership: Rediscovering the Secrets to Creating Lasting Value* (Jossey-Bass, 2003) contributed to the current popularity of that approach.

Jack Welch spoke to a standing-room-only crowd at the Harvard Business School in 1987.

"Amy's" story came from a class participant, using the framework to describe what she had done.

The 15 leadership lessons of Colin Powell, former chairman of the Joint Chiefs of Staff and former secretary of state, are found in Oren Harari's *The Leadership Secrets of Colin Powell* (McGraw-Hill Books, 2002).

One of the seminal articles on motivation is Frederick Herzberg's "One More Time: How Do You Motivate Employees?" *Harvard Business Review*, January–February 1968.

Chapter Six

Lao Tzu was a sixth-century BC Taoist philosopher credited with writing the *Tao Te Ching*. Variations on this statement are offered in many leadership articles, including Kaarina Dillabough, "Would Lao Tzu Think You're a Leader," October 17, 2013, http://changeyourgame bealeader.com/2013/10/17/lao-tzu-think-youre-leader/; and Terrence Seamon, "Leaders, Honor Thy People," January 28, 2016, http://aboutleaders.com/leaders-honor-thy-people/#gs.vpzl4Ro.

The *Globe and Mail* wrote about Linda Hasenfratz, one of the few women running a significant manufacturing business, in the June 2010 Report on Business Magazine: Dawn Calleja, "Linamar's Drive to $10-billion."

Richard Florida's *The Rise of the Creative Class* (Basic Books, 2002) was a sensation from the day it was published. A revised, 10th anniversary edition was published in 2012. Dr. Florida continues to do research and publish on the ways in which the creative class is defining work today and on the conditions that attract its members. He works out of the Martin Prosperity Institute at the Rotman School of Management.

I referred to the work of Badaracco and Ellsworth, *Leadership and the Quest for Integrity*, earlier.

James MacGregor Burns died in July 2014 at the age of 95. His life's work and his transactional/transformational concepts were celebrated in many articles at the time, including "James MacGregor Burns, Scholar of Presidents and Leadership, Dies at 95," by Bruce Weber, *New York Times*, July 15, 2014; and "Remembering James MacGregor Burns," by Jena McGregor, *Washington Post*, July 17, 2014. The book which captured his thoughts is *Leadership* (Harper and Row, 1978).

The Google story can be found in *How Google Works* by Eric Schmidt and Jonathan Rosenberg on p. 28 of the hardcover version of the book. It is regularly repeated in stories about the company.

I referred to the work of Latham and Locke earlier. Dr. Latham has also put considerable energy into making academic theory accessible to management practitioners, as with Gary P. Latham, *Becoming the Evidence-Based Manager: Making the Science of Management Work for You* (Davies-Black, 2009).

Chapter Seven

Dan Pink's thoughtful but also highly entertaining book is *Drive: The Surprising Truth About What Motivates Us* (Riverhead Books, 2009).

Simon Sinek, *Start With Why: How Great Leaders Inspire Everyone to Take Action*.

The Four Seasons and P&G sources are listed in chapter 1.

Chapter Eight

I first encountered the story of Paul Butler in *Switch: How to Change Things When Change Is Hard* by Chip Heath and Dan Heath (Random House, 2010). I have since researched the methodology behind it, which has been developed by an organization called Rare (formerly RarePlanet). Their idea is that conservation can be best achieved when it is driven by, and tuned to, the culture and the needs of local people.

The Greg Robertson story is a case study called *Great Lakes Regional Health Centre (A), (B), (C)*, written for the Rotman School of Management at the University of Toronto.

Chapter Nine

Ellen Langer has spoken at the Rotman School several times. The books that captured me are *Mindfulness* (DaCapo Books, 1990) and *Counterclockwise: Mindful Health and the Power of Possibility* (Ballantine Books, 2009).

Jonah Lehrer is a Rhodes scholar who studied neuroscience at Columbia and philosophy at Oxford. His book, *How We Decide* (Houghton Mifflin Harcourt, 2009), makes accessible a range of academic studies on the interaction between the logical and the emotional parts of the brain. Lehrer's next book was cited for plagiarism and misquotes, but there have been no allegations that *How We Decide* had any such problems. In addition, subsequent work, including *The Hour Between Dog and Wolf* by John Coates (Random House Canada, 2012), goes into further detail on the same subject.

Sheena Iyengar opens *The Art of Choosing* (Twelve, Hachette Book Group, 2010) with her own story of allowing her parents to choose her husband. The book continues to fascinate after that opening.

When Daniel Goleman's "What Makes a Leader?" was published in the *Harvard Business Review* in December 1998, the idea of emotional intelligence took center stage. He has written many books on the subject since that article. One book that captures much of his thinking is *Leadership: The Power of Emotional Intelligence: Selected Writings* (More Than Sound, 2011).

Stephane Cote's research on this topic can be found in "Emotional Intelligence and Leadership Emergence in Small Groups," *Leadership Quarterly* 21 (2010).

The idea of using a checklist for all kinds of medical activities is well summarized in Atul Gawande, "The Medical Checklist," *New Yorker*, December 10, 2007. I got a deeper insight into the medical checklist and its real-time application from a talk at the Rotman School by Dr. Bryce Taylor on April 9, 2015.

In the Remarks at the Annual Conference of the Society for Personnel Administration on May 12, 1954, Eisenhower said, "Now I think, speaking roughly, by leadership we mean the art of getting someone else to do something that you want done because he wants to do it, not because your position of power can compel him to do it, or your position of authority." My students often misquote Eisenhower in their papers, usually phrasing it "get others to do what you want done and be happy about doing it."

Bill George has written extensively on authenticity: *Authentic Leadership: Rediscovering the Secrets to Creating Lasting Value* (Jossey-Bass, 2003); with Peter Sim, *True North: Discover Your Authentic Leadership* (Jossey-Bass, 2007); *Discover Your True North* (John Wiley & Sons, 2015).

Herminia Ibarra has a different twist on authenticity in "The Authenticity Paradox," *Harvard Business Review*, January–February 2015. She argues that different situations call for different leadership responses and that leaders should not be lulled into thinking that they cannot change their habits of behaving.

ABOUT THE AUTHOR

Jim Fisher has had the good fortune of enjoying three quite separate careers. After graduating from the University of Toronto with a degree in political science and economics and serving a short stint at the Toronto-Dominion Bank, he went off to the Harvard Business School. He became a Baker scholar in his first year, graduated with high distinction, and started his first career with McKinsey and Company in their Cleveland office. He came back to Canada when they opened their Toronto office and, after two years, left with a group of colleagues to start the Canada Consulting Group. For over 15 years he was able to contribute to the great issues of the day, from the lens of either corporate strategy or public policy. Canada Consulting eventually became the Toronto office of the Boston Consulting Group.

His second career was in the food industry with George Weston Limited. As Canada phased in the North American Free Trade Agreement (NAFTA), companies like Weston had to determine which of its formerly protected businesses could be competitive in a North American context. After a few years of buying and selling various businesses, he became the president of William Neilson Limited, which included a dairy, ice cream, and chocolate confectionery business, and then president of George Weston Limited, which included the Canadian and US fresh bakery businesses with almost 8,000 employees and 23 plants from one side of North America to the other.

His third career was at the Rotman School of Management, University of Toronto. He started teaching one course while closing a small venture capital transaction. When that transaction closed, he was asked to join the school in an administrative capacity while continuing to teach his course. Over the next 15 years he became the vice dean of programs as the school grew by leaps and bounds in size and stature to become Canada's leading business school as well as a global powerhouse in academic research. His role continued to expand until he was teaching five MBA courses, winning numerous teaching awards, and working on leadership programs with many organizations.

Today he is a professor emeritus of the university, continues to teach MBA courses and executive programs, and speaks on leadership to many organizations.

INDEX

Page references followed by *fig* indicate a figure; page references followed by *t* indicate a table.